HEALTHY DISH OF THE DAY

KATE MCMILLAN

PHOTOGRAPHS BY ERIN KUNKEL

weldonowen

CONTENTS

A HEALTHY DISH FOR EVERY DAY

Lean proteins, seasonal vegetables, whole grains, and good fats—this is the formula for simple, healthy eating. A variety of colors and textures and a well-rounded plate keeps nutritious cooking interesting. Healthy eating is a way of life, one that improves your livelihood, and includes plenty of adventures in the kitchen. Balanced, seasonally inspired meals, bursting in fresh flavors and nutrients have a welcome place at the table, in any season.

With 365 recipes for every day of the year, healthy eating has never been easier. Inspired by seasonal produce, this book focuses on eating the freshest vegetables and fruits each month, ensuring variety all year long. In the colder months, keep warm and satisfied with hearty root vegetables, sturdy greens, and roasted lean meats. Celebrate the arrival of warmer months with greens, baby vegetables, and light soups. Pull out the grill for summer, and enjoy light fish dishes and plump, juicy vegetables cooked until charred and smoky.

This book will remind you that healthy eating isn't about restrictions. We've reinvented old favorites and comfort foods so they can be enjoyed in healthier forms. You'll find burgers for any season: made from fish, beans, and classic ground meat; pasta dishes galore, brimming with seasonal vegetables; casseroles composed of whole grains and hearty vegetables; and many more delicious ideas to satisfy a variety of palates.

Many recipes include serving suggestions to round out a balanced meal. You'll also find lots of recipes for simple sauces, quick garnishes, and homemade condiments to keep things interesting. Information on key nutrients is provided with many of the recipes to illuminate the health benefits that different foods offer.

With this abundance of delicious recipes, and the seasons as your guide to fresh produce, you'll be inspired to cook flavorful, fresh, and healthy meals all year long.

Resolve to eat healthy through the New Year with seasonal, satisfying meals. January is the time to fill the kitchen with root vegetables: turnips, butternut squash, carrots, and fennel bring heartiness to a cold day's meal. Complement the tender roots and squashes with warming spices, such as turmeric, cayenne, curry paste, and red pepper flakes. You can still enjoy cozy comfort foods and eat healthy by making a few alterations on classic dishes, like baked chicken Parmesan that is pan-seared instead of flour-coated, and vegetarian cassoulet that gets natural richness from a bounty of vegetables.

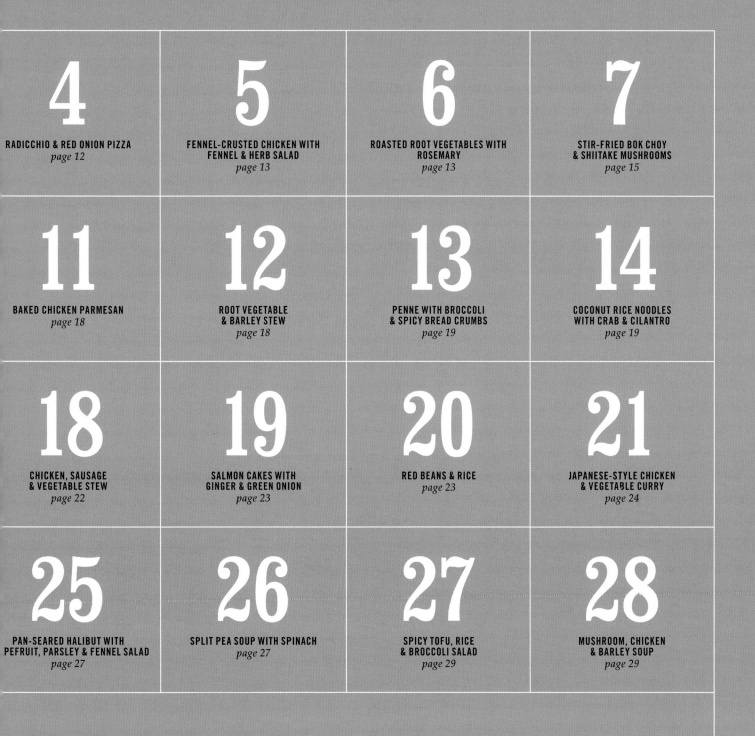

january

1

QUINOA TABBOULEH WITH LEMONY GRILLED SHRIMP

serves 4–6

1 lb (500 g) shrimp, peeled and deveined

Grated zest and juice of 1 lemon

1 tsp olive oil

Salt and freshly ground pepper

1 cup (8 oz/250 g) quinoa, rinsed

1 English cucumber, cut into ½-inch (12-mm) pieces

1 pint (12 oz/375 g) cherry tomatoes, halved

2 green onions, chopped

1 cup (1½ oz/45 g) chopped fresh flat-leaf parsley

FOR THE LEMON-GARLIC DRESSING

2 cloves garlic, minced

Juice of ½ lemon

¼ cup (2 fl oz/60 ml) extra-virgin olive oil

Salt and freshly ground pepper

Quinoa—a gluten-free, protein-packed, grain-like seed—replaces bulgur wheat in this new riff on a Mediterranean classic. The addition of low-calorie grilled shrimp makes this dish hearty enough to serve as a main course. This recipe would also be delicious with other proteins such as grilled salmon or leftover shredded rotisserie chicken.

Place the shrimp in a nonreactive bowl with the lemon zest and juice and the oil. Season with salt and pepper and toss to combine. Cover and refrigerate for 1 hour.

Bring 2 cups (16 fl oz/500 ml) water to a boil in a saucepan over medium-high heat. Add ½ tsp salt and the quinoa and reduce heat to low. Cover the saucepan and cook until the water is absorbed and the quinoa is tender, 15–20 minutes. Transfer the quinoa to a bowl and let cool.

Warm a stove-top grill pan over high heat. Remove the shrimp from the marinade and place on the grill pan; discard the marinade. Cook just until the shrimp are bright pink and opaque throughout, about 2 minutes per side. Transfer the shrimp to the bowl with the quinoa. Add the cucumber, tomatoes, green onions, and parsley and mix to combine.

To make the dressing, place the garlic and lemon juice in a small bowl. Whisk in the extra-virgin olive oil and season to taste with salt and pepper.

Stir the dressing into the quinoa. Season to taste with salt and pepper and serve at room temperature, or refrigerate and serve cold.

2

WINTER VEGETABLE CURRY

serves 4

1 Tbsp olive oil

1 large onion, finely chopped

2 serrano chiles, chopped

3 Tbsp fresh ginger, minced

1 tsp cumin seeds

2 cans (15 oz/470 g each) chickpeas, liquid reserved

1 can (14.5 oz/455 g) diced tomatoes

1 Tbsp fresh lime juice

¼ tsp ground turmeric

¾ tsp garam masala

½ large cauliflower, cut into 1-inch (2.5-cm) florets

2 Yukon gold potatoes, cut into ½-inch (12-mm) pieces

Salt and freshly ground pepper

Cooked brown rice, for serving

⅓ cup (½ oz/15 g) minced fresh cilantro

This vegetarian curry has all the elements of a complete meal: vegetables for vitamins and minerals, chickpeas for plant-based protein, and brown rice, a source of whole grains and a vehicle for mopping up the fragrant curry sauce. This stew reheats well, so it can be served again a night or two later.

In a heavy large saucepan over medium-high heat, warm the oil. Add the onion, chiles, ginger, and cumin seeds. Sauté until the onion is tender, about 6 minutes. Add the chickpeas with their liquid, tomatoes with their juice, lime juice, turmeric, and ½ tsp garam masala. Bring to a boil, then reduce the heat and simmer for 5 minutes to blend the flavors.

Add the cauliflower, potatoes, and 1 cup (8 fl oz/250 ml) water, and simmer until the potatoes are tender, stirring occasionally and adding more water if dry, about 15 minutes. Stir in the remaining ¼ tsp garam masala. Season to taste with salt and pepper.

Spoon the curry over rice in bowls, sprinkle with cilantro, and serve.

3

This minestrone is made healthy by bolstering it with extra vegetables, mainly vitamin C-dense cabbage, and using a low-sodium broth base. The key to perfecting this soup is to cut all the vegetables into similar size chunks so that they cook evenly.

MINESTRONE

serves 4–6

1 cup (7 oz/220 g) dried cannellini beans

3 large leeks

1 large fennel bulb

2 carrots

Salt and freshly ground pepper

1 bay leaf, preferably fresh

¾ cup (2 oz/60 g) tubetti or other small pasta

5 Tbsp (2½ fl oz/75 ml) extra-virgin olive oil, plus more for drizzling

3 thin slices pancetta, finely chopped

2 cloves garlic, crushed

1 cup (3 oz/90 g) thinly sliced savoy cabbage

2 Tbsp finely chopped fresh rosemary

2 tomatoes, peeled, seeded, and chopped

6 cups (48 fl oz/1.5 l) low-sodium chicken broth

2 Tbsp chopped fresh flat-leaf parsley

½ cup (2 oz/60 g) freshly grated pecorino romano cheese

Pick over the beans and discard any broken beans or grit. Rinse the beans well, place in a bowl, add water to cover by 2 inches (5 cm), and soak overnight.

Drain the beans and place in a large pot. Add water to cover by about 3 inches (7.5 cm).

Trim the leeks (you want the white and pale green parts only), fennel, and carrots, reserving all the trimmings. Finely dice the vegetables. Add the vegetable trimmings to the pot with the beans along with a pinch of salt and the bay leaf. Bring to a boil, reduce the heat to low, cover, and simmer gently until the beans are tender, about 1 hour. Meanwhile, cook the pasta in a large pot of salted water until al dente, 8–10 minutes. Drain and toss with 2 Tbsp of the oil.

In a large pot over medium heat, warm the remaining 3 Tbsp oil. Add the pancetta and sauté until crisp, about 4 minutes. Add the diced vegetables, season with salt and pepper, and sauté until the vegetables are starting to soften, about 5 minutes. Add the garlic and sauté for 1 minute. Add the cabbage and rosemary and sauté for about 1 minute. Add the tomatoes and broth and bring to a boil. Remove the vegetable trimmings and bay leaf from the beans ⟫→

and add the beans with their liquid to the soup pot. Reduce the heat to low and simmer until the vegetables are very tender, 15–20 minutes. Add the pasta and parsley and warm through. Adjust the seasoning.

Ladle the soup into bowls, drizzle with olive oil, sprinkle with cheese, and serve.

4

Whole wheat dough, a light scattering of cheese, and a hearty serving of vegetables makes this pizza a healthier choice than a classic cheesy pie. Caramelized and crisped, these antioxidant-rich vegetables bring striking purple hues to a blank pizza canvas.

RADICCHIO & RED ONION PIZZA

serves 2–4

1 Tbsp extra-virgin olive oil, plus more for brushing

2 red onions, thinly sliced

1 lb (500 g) purchased whole-wheat pizza dough

Flour and cornmeal, for dusting

2 garlic cloves, minced

½ cup (2 oz/60 g) shredded fontina cheese

1½ cups (4½ oz/140 g) thinly sliced radicchio

½ cup (2 oz/60 g) grated Parmesan cheese

Red pepper flakes

Salt

Position a rack in the bottom of the oven. Place a baking stone on the rack. Preheat the oven to 550°F (290°C), or the highest setting, for at least 45 minutes.

In a large frying pan over medium heat, warm the 1 Tbsp olive oil. Add the onions and sauté until tender, about 8 minutes.

To assemble the pizza, lightly flour a work surface. Roll out the dough into a round 13–14 inches (33–35 cm) in diameter. Generously dust a pizza peel or rimless baking sheet with cornmeal and transfer the dough round to it. Working quickly, brush the dough with olive oil. Spread the garlic over the dough, then sprinkle evenly with the fontina, sautéed onions, and radicchio. Sprinkle with the Parmesan and red pepper flakes to taste, then season with salt.

Immediately slide the pizza from the peel or baking sheet onto the baking stone. Bake until the crust is crisp and browned, about 10 minutes. Remove from the oven. Brush the rim of the crust with the oil, and serve.

5

FENNEL–CRUSTED CHICKEN WITH FENNEL & HERB SALAD

serves 2

1½ tsp fennel seeds

¼ tsp black peppercorns

Salt and freshly ground black pepper

⅛ tsp red pepper flakes

2 boneless, skinless chicken breast halves

4 tsp extra-virgin olive oil

½ small fennel bulb, shaved (about ½ cup/ 2 oz/60 g), plus 1 Tbsp fennel fronds

2 Tbsp chopped fresh chives

2 Tbsp fresh flat-leaf parsley leaves

1 Tbsp fresh lemon juice

¼ cup (2 fl oz/60 ml) dry rosé wine

¼ cup (2 fl oz/60 ml) low-sodium chicken broth

An herb salad is a quick fix for meals that need color and added nutrients. Often more dense in nutrients than light-colored lettuces, herbs are a nice break from the ordinary when served as a side dish.

In a mortar using a pestle, grind together the fennel seeds, peppercorns, ¼ tsp salt, and red pepper flakes until coarsely ground.

Place 1 chicken breast half between 2 sheets of plastic wrap and pound lightly with a meat mallet until evenly flattened to ½-inch (12-mm) thick. Repeat with the second chicken breast.

In a large frying pan over medium-high heat, warm 2 tsp of the oil. Sprinkle both sides of the chicken breasts evenly with the fennel seed mixture. Cook, turning once, until golden brown on both sides and just cooked through, 3–4 minutes on each side.

Meanwhile, stir together the shaved fennel, chives, parsley, fennel fronds, lemon juice, and the remaining oil in a medium bowl and season to taste with salt and black pepper.

Transfer the chicken breasts to warmed plates. Add the wine and broth to the frying pan and simmer until reduced by about half, about 1 minute. Pour the pan juices over the chicken and top each with some of the fennel-herb salad, dividing evenly, and serve.

6

ROASTED ROOT VEGETABLES WITH ROSEMARY

serves 4–6

½ lb (250 g) red boiling onions

1 large or 2 small heads garlic

4 large carrots, peeled and cut into large chunks

2 large parsnips, peeled, cut into large chunks, and any tough cores cut away

3 golden beets, peeled and cut into large wedges

2 rutabagas, peeled and cut into large wedges

5 red potatoes, scrubbed and cut into large chunks

⅓ cup (3 fl oz/80 ml) olive oil

Salt and freshly ground pepper

2 long sprigs fresh rosemary, cut in half

Leaves from 6–8 sprigs fresh flat-leaf parsley, chopped

Skip the rosemary and try an arugula-mint pesto in it's place. In a blender, combine 5 cups (5 oz/155 g) packed arugula, ¾ cup (½ oz/15 g) packed fresh mint leaves, ½ cup (4 fl oz/ 125 ml) extra-virgin olive oil, ½ cup (2 oz/60 g) Parmesan cheese, 2 cloves garlic, grated zest of 1 lemon, and salt and pepper to taste and blend until smooth. Stir in 1 Tbsp lemon juice and adjust the seasoning. Refrigerate until ready to serve. The pesto can be used as a dip or mixed in with the vegetables.

Position a rack in the center of the oven and preheat the oven to 425°F (220°C).

Bring a saucepan three-fourths full of water to a boil. Add the onions to the boiling water and cook for about 1 minute, then drain into a colander and rinse under running cold water. Using a paring knife, trim away the small root ends. Ease the onions from their outer skins with your fingers.

Slice the top ½ inch (12 mm) off the head(s) of garlic to expose the cloves, and rub off any loose outer papery skins. Put the carrots, parsnips, beets, rutabagas, potatoes, and garlic head(s) in a large bowl. Add the olive oil, 1 tsp salt, and ¼ tsp pepper and toss to coat. Arrange the vegetables in a single layer in a large, heavy-duty roasting pan. Tuck 2 of the rosemary sprigs among the vegetables. Pour 1 cup (8 fl oz/250 ml) water into the pan and roast, stirring every 20 minutes or so, until the vegetables are golden and the biggest pieces are tender when pierced with the tip of a knife, 1–1½ hours.

Mince the remaining rosemary and mix it with the parsley. When the vegetables are done, transfer them to a warmed platter. Set the garlic heads upright among the vegetables. Season the vegetables with salt and pepper, sprinkle with the parsley and rosemary, and serve.

7

STIR-FRIED BOK CHOY & SHIITAKE MUSHROOMS

serves 4

¼ cup (2 fl oz/60 ml) low-sodium chicken broth

1 Tbsp Chinese rice wine

1 Tbsp oyster sauce

1 Tbsp ginger juice

1 tsp Asian sesame oil

½ tsp sugar

½ tsp cornstarch

1 lb (500 g) bok choy

8 shiitake mushrooms

3 Tbsp grapeseed oil

4 cloves garlic

Cooked brown rice, for serving

Every home cook needs a great go-to stir-fry recipe. This one is fresh, quick, and nutritious—everything a stir-fry should be. Ginger juice can be extracted from finely grated fresh ginger or found in store-bought jars of minced or chopped ginger. If you like, add cubed tofu for additional protein.

In a small bowl, whisk together the broth, rice wine, oyster sauce, ginger juice, sesame oil, sugar, and cornstarch to make a sauce.

Trim the stem ends from the bok choy, then cut each bunch lengthwise into quarters. Remove the stems from the mushrooms and discard. Cut the caps in half.

In a wok over high heat, warm 1 Tbsp of the grapeseed oil. Add 2 of the garlic cloves and stir-fry until golden brown, about 20 seconds. Discard the garlic. Quickly add half of the bok choy to the hot pan and stir-fry until just wilted, 3–4 minutes. Transfer to a colander. Add 1 Tbsp grapeseed oil to the pan and stir-fry the remaining garlic and bok choy in the same manner. Set the bok choy aside in the colander to drain. In the same pan over high heat, warm the remaining 1 Tbsp grapeseed oil. Add the mushrooms and sauté until they release their juices, 4–5 minutes.

Return the bok choy to the pan, add the sauce, and stir-fry until the sauce has thickened slightly, 1–2 minutes longer. Serve over brown rice.

8

ASIAN-STYLE CHICKEN SOUP

serves 4

8 cups (64 fl oz/2 l) low-sodium chicken broth

1 bunch green onions, plus thinly sliced green onions for serving

2-inch (5-cm) piece fresh ginger, peeled and sliced

2 Tbsp Asian fish sauce

1 Tbsp sugar

6 *each* star anise pods and cloves

1–1¼ lb (500–625 g) skinless, boneless chicken breasts

3 Thai chiles, or 1 serrano chile, thinly sliced

Bean sprouts, basil sprigs, cilantro sprigs, and lime wedges for serving

Hoisin sauce (optional)

4 heads baby bok choy

6–7 oz (185–220 g) dried rice stick noodles

Salt and freshly ground pepper

Here, chicken, vegetables, and rice noodles are cooked in a clear, spice-infused broth. An abundance of bright green garnishes liven up this one-dish meal. The more green you add, the healthier and more flavorful this soup becomes.

In a large pot over high heat, combine the broth and 2 cups (16 fl oz/500 ml) water. Cut the green onion bunch in half crosswise and add to the pot; add the ginger, fish sauce, and sugar. In a tea ball, combine the star anise and cloves; add to the pot. Bring the broth to a boil. Add the chicken breasts, return to a boil, reduce the heat to medium-low, and simmer until the chicken is cooked through, 10–15 minutes. Using tongs, transfer the chicken to a plate. Continue to simmer the broth to develop the flavor, 15–30 minutes.

Place the sliced green onions, sliced chiles, bean sprouts, herb sprigs, lime wedges, and hoisin sauce, if using, on a platter and set on the table.

Slice the bok choy crosswise about ½ inch (12 mm) thick. Thinly slice the chicken breasts crosswise. In a large bowl, soak the noodles in very hot water for 3 minutes.

Remove the green onions and ginger from the broth and discard. Season the broth to taste with salt and pepper. Add the bok choy, raise the heat to high, and bring to a boil. Drain the noodles, add them to the broth, and cook until just tender, about 2 minutes.

Using tongs, divide the noodles and bok choy among 4 warmed deep bowls. Divide the chicken among the bowls. Ladle the broth over the top. Serve, allowing diners to add the condiments to taste.

9

Tri-tip is a full-flavored cut of meat that remains juicy and moist even when trimmed of fat. Brussels sprouts are full of vitamins to enrich this meal even more. To round out your plate, try roasting baby potatoes at the same time as the vegetables.

SPICED TRI-TIP WITH ROASTED BRUSSELS SPROUTS

serves 4–6

2 lb (1 kg) beef tri-tip, trimmed of fat

Salt and freshly ground pepper

2¼ tsp sweet paprika

2 tsp caraway seeds

2 tsp dried marjoram

1 tsp dry mustard

½ tsp cayenne pepper

3½ Tbsp olive oil, plus more for brushing

1 lb (500 g) brussels sprouts, halved lengthwise

¾ lb (375 g) small shallots, halved lengthwise, plus 1 large shallot, minced

1 Tbsp low-sodium soy sauce, plus 2 tsp

½ cup (4 fl oz/125 ml) dry vermouth

½ cup (4 fl oz/125 ml) low-sodium beef or chicken broth

2 tsp unsalted butter

Preheat the oven to 450°F (230°C). Season the beef with salt and pepper, and place on a baking rack set in a shallow roasting pan.

Mix together 2 tsp of the paprika, 1 tsp of the caraway seeds, ½ tsp of the marjoram, the mustard, and cayenne. Mix in 1 Tbsp of the oil, then rub the mixture all over the beef. Oil a large baking pan and add the brussels sprouts, halved shallots, the 1 Tbsp soy sauce, plus the remaining 2½ Tbsp oil, 1 tsp caraway seeds, and 1 tsp marjoram. Mix to coat. Roast the beef and vegetables until an instant-read thermometer inserted in the thickest part of the beef registers 120°F (49°C) for rare, about 20 minutes, or until cooked to your liking. Roast the vegetables until tender and browned, about 25 minutes. Remove the beef from the oven, transfer to a warmed platter, tent with foil, and let rest for 15 minutes.

Spoon 1 Tbsp fat from the roasting pan into a saucepan over medium heat; discard the remaining fat. Add the minced shallot to the saucepan and sauté until it begins to soften, about 1 minute. Add the vermouth to the roasting pan, set it over medium-high heat, and bring to a boil, scraping up the browned bits on the pan bottom. Pour the mixture into the saucepan and boil until syrupy, ⟩⟩→

about 3 minutes. Add the broth, remaining ¼ tsp paprika, and 2 tsp soy sauce to the pan. Boil the sauce until syrupy, about 5 minutes. Remove the pan from the heat and pour in any juices from the platter. Whisk in the butter and the remaining ½ tsp marjoram. Season with salt and pepper. Slice the beef and arrange on a warmed platter with the vegetables. Serve with the sauce.

10

Lacinato kale, also referred to as dinosaur kale, is the mildest variety of kale. It still delivers an abundance of nutrients, but without the bitter kale taste found in other varieties. Lightly massaging the vinaigrette into the leaves helps soften their texture and allows the flavors to soak in. Pancetta is used sparingly for a touch of meatiness.

KALE SALAD WITH RADICCHIO & PANCETTA

serves 4

3 thin slices (1½ oz/45 g) pancetta

2 Tbsp extra-virgin olive oil

1 Tbsp balsamic vinegar

1 Tbsp fresh lemon juice

1 clove garlic, minced

¼ tsp salt

1 bunch lacinato or other kale (about 1 lb/500 g)

1 small head radicchio, torn into small pieces

¼ cup (1½ oz) grated pecorino romano cheese

Freshly ground pepper

In a large, heavy frying pan over medium heat, fry the pancetta until crisp, turning once, about 8 minutes. Transfer the pancetta to a plate to cool.

In a large bowl, whisk together the oil, vinegar, lemon juice, garlic, and salt. Using a sharp knife, remove the center ribs from the kale leaves and discard. Stack the leaves, roll them into a cylinder, and cut crosswise into strips. Add the kale and radicchio to the bowl and toss until coated, massaging the leaves with your hands until the kale is wilted and tender.

Crumble the pancetta over the salad. Add the cheese, season with pepper, and toss to combine. Serve.

11

BAKED CHICKEN PARMESAN

serves 4

Classic comfort food gets a healthy treatment in this low-fat version of chicken Parmesan. We took away the heavy flour coating and replaced it with a natural pan-seared crust thanks to a quick stint on the stove before finishing in the oven. The addition of fibrous kale makes a balanced meal.

4 boneless, skinless chicken breast halves, about 1½ lb (750 g) total weight

Salt and freshly ground pepper

2 Tbsp olive oil

1 bunch kale, leaves stripped from stems and torn into large pieces

2 cups (16 fl oz/500 ml) prepared marinara sauce, warmed

4 slices fresh mozzarella cheese, ¼ inch (6 mm) thick

¼ cup (1 oz/30 g) freshly grated Parmesan cheese

Preheat the oven to 400°F (200°C). Season the chicken generously on all sides with salt and pepper.

In a large ovenproof frying pan over medium-high heat, warm the oil. Add the chicken and cook, turning once, until golden brown, about 7 minutes total. Transfer to a plate and set aside.

Add the kale to the pan and sauté over medium-high heat until wilted, about 1 minute. Return the chicken to the frying pan with the kale and pour over the marinara sauce. Place 2 cheese slices on each chicken breast. Sprinkle evenly with the Parmesan cheese. Bake until the cheese is golden and the chicken is opaque throughout, about 20 minutes.

Let stand for about 5 minutes, and serve.

12

ROOT VEGETABLE & BARLEY STEW

serves 6

This wintery stew will fuel you with its healthy measure of complex carbohydrates. Jerusalem artichokes, sometimes called sunchokes, are an excellent source of iron. If you have trouble finding them, add an additional potato or another favorite root vegetable in their place.

6 Tbsp (3 fl oz/90 ml) extra-virgin olive oil

1 yellow onion, finely chopped

1 carrot, peeled and finely chopped

1 celery stalk, finely chopped

1 cup (8 fl oz/250 ml) dry white wine

5½ cups (44 fl oz/1.3 l) low-sodium vegetable broth

½ cup (4 oz/125 g) pearl barley

¼ cup (⅓ oz/10 g) minced fresh flat-leaf parsley

2 tsp minced fresh thyme

1 celery root, peeled and diced

½ lb (250 g) Jerusalem artichokes, peeled and quartered

3 parsnips, peeled and thinly sliced crosswise

1 red onion, cut into 1-inch (2.5-cm) pieces

1 large red potato, unpeeled, cut into 1-inch (2.5-cm) pieces

Salt and freshly ground pepper

Preheat the oven to 400°F (200°C). Lightly oil a baking sheet.

In a large saucepan over medium-high heat, warm 3 tablespoons of the olive oil. Add the yellow onion, carrot, and celery and sauté until browned, 7–8 minutes. Raise the heat to high, add the wine, and stir with a wooden spoon to scrape up the browned bits from the pan bottom. Continue to cook until the wine is reduced by one-half, about 5 minutes.

Add the broth and bring to a boil over high heat. Add the barley, parsley, and thyme and reduce the heat to medium-low. Simmer for 35 minutes. Add the celery root, Jerusalem artichokes, and parsnips. Cover and cook over medium-low heat until the vegetables are tender, 15–20 minutes longer.

In a large bowl, combine the red onion, potato, and remaining 3 tablespoons olive oil. Toss to coat well. Spread on the prepared baking sheet and sprinkle with salt. Roast until the vegetables are browned and tender, 40–45 minutes.

Add the vegetables to the pot and stir well. Season with salt and pepper, and serve.

PENNE WITH BROCCOLI & SPICY BREAD CRUMBS

serves 4

Hearty and healthy, this pasta dish delivers comforting flavors, like a crispy bread crumb crust, and nutritious elements, like tender broccoli. You can omit the anchovies, if desired, and add something else salty, such as chopped olives or capers.

FOR THE SPICY BREAD CRUMBS

2 Tbsp extra-virgin olive oil

¾ cup (1½ oz/45 g) coarse fresh bread crumbs made from coarse country whole-wheat bread

Generous pinch of red pepper flakes

Salt

Leaves from 2 fresh oregano sprigs

1 large bunch broccoli (about 1½ lb/750 g)

1 lb (500 g) dried penne or rigatoni

2 Tbsp extra-virgin olive oil

5 cloves garlic, thinly sliced

6 anchovy fillets, finely chopped

Pinch of red pepper flakes

¼ cup (2 fl oz/60 ml) dry white wine

To make the bread crumbs, in a small frying pan over medium heat, warm 2 Tbsp oil. Add the bread crumbs, pepper flakes, salt to taste, and oregano and sauté until the crumbs are lightly golden, about 4 minutes.

Bring a large pot of water to a boil. Cut the broccoli into small florets and thinly slice the tender parts of the stems. Generously salt the water, add the broccoli, and cook for 2 minutes. Scoop the broccoli from the pot with a skimmer and place in a colander. Rinse well under cold water and drain well. Return the water to a boil, add the pasta, and cook until al dente, 10–12 minutes.

Meanwhile, in a large frying pan over medium heat, warm 2 Tbsp oil. Add the garlic and anchovies and sauté until the garlic is lightly golden, 1–2 minutes. Add the broccoli, pepper flakes, and salt to taste and sauté for 2–3 minutes. Add the wine and cook until nearly evaporated, 1–2 minutes.

Drain the pasta, reserving about ¾ cup (6 fl oz/178 ml) of the cooking water, and add ½ cup (4 fl oz/125 ml) water to the pan with the broccoli. Toss quickly over medium heat to mix well. Add the reserved pasta water as needed to loosen the sauce. Taste and adjust the seasoning. Transfer to a warmed large, shallow bowl, sprinkle with the bread crumbs, and serve.

COCONUT RICE NOODLES WITH CRAB & CILANTRO

serves 4

Using coconut milk is a great way to add natural creaminess and nutrients to a meal. It's easier to digest than dairy milk and helps maintain the Asian integrity of these noodles. Lime juice and coconut milk are a timeless combination that brings fresh flavor to this dish.

Salt

½ lb (250 g) dried flat rice noodles, about ¼ inch (6 mm) wide

¼ cup (2 fl oz/60 ml) unsweetened coconut milk

2–3 Tbsp Asian fish sauce

2 Tbsp fresh lime juice

Grated zest of 1 lime

2–4 Thai chiles, sliced (optional)

1 cup (1 oz/30 g) mung bean sprouts

½ English cucumber, cut into paper-thin slices

½ lb (250 g) fresh lump crabmeat, picked over for shell fragments and cartilage and flaked

½ cup (½ oz/15 g) fresh cilantro leaves

In a large pot, bring 4 qt (4 l) water to a rapid boil. Add 1 tablespoon salt and the noodles, stir well, and cook, stirring occasionally, until just tender, 3–5 minutes. Drain in a colander, place under cold running water to cool, and drain again thoroughly.

In a bowl, stir together the coconut milk, fish sauce to taste, lime juice, lime zest, and chiles to taste, if using. Add the bean sprouts, cucumber, and crabmeat and toss gently to mix.

Transfer the noodles to a large, shallow serving bowl. Arrange the crab mixture over the noodles. Scatter the cilantro on top. Serve at room temperature, or cover and refrigerate for up to 3 hours and serve chilled.

15

CHICKEN WITH SQUASH, TURNIPS & SHIITAKES

serves 4

2 Tbsp olive oil

¼ lb (625 g) boneless, skinless chicken thighs

Salt and freshly ground pepper

1 large yellow onion, finely chopped

1 Tbsp fresh sage, minced

1 lb (500 g) butternut squash, peeled, seeded, and cut into ½-inch (12-mm) pieces

2 bunches small turnips, unpeeled, cut into ½-inch (12-mm) pieces, greens reserved

1½ cups (12 fl oz/375 ml) low-sodium chicken broth, plus 1 Tbsp

½ lb (250 g) shiitake mushrooms, stemmed and cut into 1-inch (2.5-cm) pieces

1½ tsp all-purpose flour

Braising chicken with vegetables and herbs is a great way of getting ingredients to mingle and form something more delicious than the sum of their parts. Here, squash, turnips, and mushrooms add deep flavor to chicken thighs. Serve over brown rice to absorb all the savory juices of this dish.

In a large, heavy frying pan over medium-high heat, warm 1 Tbsp oil. Season the chicken with salt and pepper. Add the chicken to the pan and cook until browned, about 1½ minutes on each side. Using tongs, transfer the chicken to a plate. Reduce the heat to medium; add the onion and sage to the pan, and sauté until tender, about 5 minutes. Add the squash and turnips, and stir to coat with oil. Add 1½ cups (12 fl oz/375 ml) broth. Bring to a boil, reduce the heat to medium-low, cover, and simmer until the vegetables are tender, about 25 minutes.

Meanwhile, in a large frying pan over medium-high heat, warm the remaining 1 Tbsp oil. Add the mushrooms, season with salt and pepper, and sauté until tender, about 3 minutes. Remove from the heat. Chop half of the turnip greens, reserving the remainder for another use. Add the mushrooms and chopped turnip greens to the chicken. Cover and simmer until the greens wilt, about 5 minutes.

Put the flour in a small bowl and gradually whisk in the remaining 1 Tbsp broth until smooth. Add to the pan, stirring; cover, and simmer until the sauce thickens, about 2 minutes. Adjust the seasoning, and serve.

16

MAHIMAHI WITH MANGO SALSA

serves 4

4 mahimahi steaks, each about 6 oz (185 g) and 1-inch (2.5-cm) thick

1 Tbsp oyster sauce

2 tsp grated fresh ginger

1 Tbsp grapeseed or canola oil, plus additional for greasing

1 large just-ripe mango, peeled, pitted, and finely chopped

1 small red chile, seeded and minced

2 Tbsp chopped fresh cilantro

2 Tbsp lime juice

Salt and freshly ground pepper

Mahimahi has a mild and sweet taste when cooked. It's great for grilling or pan-frying because the steaks remain firm and not flaky. Mango is bursting with vitamins A and C and makes a vibrant salsa atop grilled white fish. This dish pairs beautifully with a simple green salad.

Place the fish steaks in a shallow dish. In a small bowl, whisk together the oyster sauce, ginger, and oil to make a marinade. Pour the marinade over the fish and turn to coat. Cover and refrigerate for 1–4 hours.

In a small bowl, combine the mango, chile, cilantro, and lime juice, and stir to mix well. Season with salt and a generous amount of pepper, then cover and refrigerate until ready to serve, up to 8 hours.

Warm a stove-top grill pan over medium-high heat. Oil the pan well. Grill the steaks, turning once, until seared and browned but still slightly translucent in the center, 3–4 minutes per side. Transfer to a platter, tent with foil, and let rest for 5 minutes.

Serve the fish topped with the mango salsa.

17

ROASTED CAULIFLOWER PASTA WITH GARLIC BREAD CRUMBS

serves 4–6

This dish has the hallmarks of any memorable pasta dish: a pleasing variety of textures and vivid, complementary flavors. Roasting cauliflower caramelizes the vegetable and brings out its natural sweetness. The penne can be omitted for a lighter vegetable side dish.

4 slices artisan-style whole-wheat bread, each about ½-inch (12-mm) thick

2 cloves garlic, peeled

2 heads (about 2 lb/1 kg) cauliflower

3 Tbsp olive oil

Salt

¾ lb (375 g) whole-wheat penne

¼ cup (2 fl oz/60 ml) lemon juice

¼ cup (⅓ oz/10 g) chopped fresh parsley

3 Tbsp capers, drained

1 tsp red pepper flakes

¼ cup (1 oz/30 g) grated Parmesan cheese

Preheat the oven to 300°F (150°C). Place the bread on a baking sheet and bake until crisp and dry, about 30 minutes. Rub one side of each slice with a garlic clove. Cool, then tear into chunks. Put in a food processor and process into coarse crumbs. Increase the oven temperature to 400°F (200°C).

Cut the cauliflower into quarters. Discard the leaves and cores and cut into ¼- to ½-inch (6- to 12-mm) slices. Mince the remaining garlic. Put the cauliflower in a large baking pan and gently toss with the oil, ½ tsp salt, and the minced garlic. Roast, stirring after 10 minutes, until cauliflower is browned on edges and tender when pierced, about 20 minutes.

Cook the pasta in a large pot of salted water until al dente, about 12 minutes or according to package directions. Drain, reserving ½ cup (4 fl oz/125 ml) of the pasta cooking water. Return the pasta to the pot and mix with the cauliflower, lemon juice, parsley, capers, red pepper flakes, and the reserved cooking water. Stir in the bread crumbs and cheese, and serve.

18

CHICKEN, SAUSAGE & VEGETABLE STEW

serves 8

This hearty stew gets rich flavor from sweet paprika, spicy turkey sausage (a lower fat alternative to pork sausage), and herbs. Brimming in tender vegetables and potates, this dish is a healthy way of satisfying a meat-and-potatoes craving. To reduce the overall fat content, pull the skin off the chicken pieces after browning them.

4 skinless chicken breast halves, thighs, and drumsticks (12 pieces total)

1 Tbsp sweet paprika

2 Tbsp olive oil

Salt and freshly ground pepper

¼ lb (125 g) hot Italian turkey sausages

10–12 baby carrots

1 yellow onion, chopped

2 Tbsp all-purpose flour

1½ cups (12 fl oz/375 ml) low-sodium chicken broth

1½ cups (12 fl oz/375 ml) dry white wine

2 cups (10 oz/300 g) butternut squash cubes

10 small red potatoes

2 tsp dried thyme

½ lb (250 g) cremini mushrooms, sliced

Sprinkle the chicken with the paprika. In a Dutch oven over high heat, warm the oil. In batches, cook the chicken, turning once, until well browned, about 2 minutes on each side. Transfer to a plate and season with salt and pepper.

Reduce the heat to medium and add the sausages to the pan. Cook until browned on all sides, about 4 minutes total. Transfer the sausages to a cutting board and, when cool enough to handle, slice into rounds ½ inch (12 mm) thick.

Raise the heat to medium-high, add the carrots and onion to the pan, and sauté until the onion is softened, about 4 minutes. Stir in the flour and sauté for 1 minute. Add the broth and scrape up the browned bits. Add the wine, squash, potatoes, and thyme.

Return the chicken and sausage to the pot, season with salt and pepper, and bring to a simmer. Add half of the mushrooms, reduce the heat to medium-low, cover partially, and simmer until the chicken juices run clear when pierced and the potatoes are tender, about 20 minutes. Stir in the remaining mushrooms and cook until tender, 5–10 minutes longer.

Ladle the stew into warmed bowls to serve.

19

SALMON CAKES WITH GINGER & GREEN ONION

serves 4

These crisp fish cakes are chock-full of good-for-you fats and savory Asian flavors. This memorable dish is wonderful served with steamed bok choy and brown rice.

2 Tbsp coarsely chopped fresh ginger

2 green onions, white and pale green parts, coarsely chopped

1 lb (500 g) wild salmon fillet, skin removed, cut into small pieces

1 tsp cornstarch

1 large egg white

Salt

1 tsp Asian fish sauce

1 Tbsp canola oil, or as needed

1 Tbsp sesame seeds, toasted

Low-sodium soy sauce, for serving

Sriracha sauce, for serving

1 lime, cut into wedges

In a food processor, combine the ginger and green onions and process until finely chopped, stopping once or twice to scrape down the sides of the work bowl. Sprinkle the salmon with the cornstarch and add to the processor with the egg white, a pinch of salt, and the fish sauce. Using quick pulses, process until the mixture resembles coarsely ground meat. Do not overprocess or the cakes will be heavy.

Divide the salmon mixture into 8 equal portions. With moistened hands, gently shape each portion into a patty about ½ inch (12 mm) thick. Transfer to a plate, cover with plastic wrap, and refrigerate for 5–10 minutes.

In a large frying pan over medium heat, warm the 1 Tbsp oil. Add the salmon cakes and cook until golden brown on the first side, about 3 minutes. Turn, adding more oil if needed, and cook until the cakes are slightly springy to the touch and have lost their raw color in the center, 2–3 minutes longer. Transfer to plates and sprinkle with the sesame seeds. Serve, passing the soy sauce, Sriracha sauce, and lime wedges at the table.

20

RED BEANS & RICE

serves 6

This is a modified verion of a staple Cuban dish that substitutes whole-grain brown rice for traditional white rice. Bacon is used in moderation for a smoky flavor. The real seasoning superstars are the herbs and spices. Cumin is known to boost immune health and aid digestion.

1 cup (7 oz/220 g) dried red beans

1 dried bay leaf

Salt and freshly ground pepper

2 tsp olive oil

2 strips thick-sliced bacon, diced

½ white onion, diced

½ *each* green and red bell pepper, seeded and diced

2 cloves garlic, minced

2 tsp *each* dried oregano and ground cumin

1 can (8 fl oz/250 ml) tomato sauce

1½ cups (10½ oz/330 g) long-grain brown rice

2½ cups (20 fl oz/625 ml) low-sodium chicken broth or water

Pick over the beans and discard any broken beans or grit. Rinse the beans well, place in a bowl, add water to cover by 2 inches (5 cm), and soak overnight.

Drain the beans and place in a large pot. Add the bay leaf and 8 cups (80 fl oz/2 l) water and bring to a boil over high heat. Reduce the heat to low and simmer for 1 hour. Add 1 tsp salt and simmer until the beans are very tender, 2–3 hours. Remove from the heat and let the beans cool in their liquid.

In a heavy frying pan over medium heat, warm the olive oil. Add the bacon and sauté until crisp, about 8 minutes. Add the onion, bell peppers, and garlic and sauté until the vegetables are softened, about 2 minutes. Add the oregano, cumin, and ½ tsp pepper and cook for 1 minute. Add the tomato sauce and cook until most of the liquid has evaporated, about 5 minutes longer. Add the rice and stir until the rice is coated and has absorbed the tomato mixture. Add the broth, stir once, and bring to a boil. Reduce the heat to low, cover, and cook until the rice has absorbed all of the liquid, 40–45 minutes.

Spoon the beans, along with a few spoonfuls of the cooking liquid, into the pan with the rice and mix. Cover and cook until the rice has absorbed all of the liquid from the beans, about 10 minutes. Remove from the heat and let stand, covered, for 5 minutes, then stir gently. Season to taste with salt. Divide among warmed bowls or plates and serve.

21

JAPANESE-STYLE CHICKEN & VEGETABLE CURRY

serves 6

12 oz (375 g) Japanese udon noodles

2 tsp curry powder

Salt and freshly ground pepper

½ lb (375 g) boneless, skinless chicken breast, cut into bite-size pieces

2 Tbsp peanut oil

¾ cup (3 oz/90 g) carrot rounds (¼-inch/6-mm thick rounds)

¾ cup (3 oz/90 g) parsnip rounds (¼-inch/6-mm thick rounds)

½ cup (2 oz/60 g) thinly sliced onions

2 cups (16 fl oz/500 ml) low-sodium chicken broth

2 tsp low-sodium soy sauce

2 tsp cornstarch

½ cup (2 oz/60 g) peeled and grated apple

This dish plays on a few different cuisine staples and brings them together in one bowl, brimming with flavor. Crisp apples top off the silky noodles with spiced chicken and vegetables. Peanut oil is a good alternative to olive oil—it's still full of healthy fat, but imparts a unique nutty flavor.

Bring a large pot of generously salted water to a boil over high heat. Add the udon and cook until just tender, 3–5 minutes. Drain well, rinse under cold running water, and set aside.

In a small sauté pan, toast the curry powder over medium heat until just fragrant, about 1 minute. Transfer to a bowl and add 2 tsp salt and ½ tsp pepper. Mix well to combine. Add the chicken pieces and toss to coat.

In a wok over medium-high heat, warm 1 Tbsp of the oil. Add the chicken and stir-fry until lightly browned, 3–4 minutes. Remove the chicken from the pan and set aside. Add the remaining 1 Tbsp oil to the wok, reduce the heat to medium, and stir in the carrots, parsnips, and onion. Stir-fry the vegetables until just tender with a bit of a bite, 4–6 minutes.

In a bowl, stir together the broth, soy sauce, and cornstarch until dissolved. Add the mixture to the wok, along with the chicken and the apple. Increase the heat to high and cook, stirring, until the sauce begins to thicken. Reduce the heat to medium-low and cook, stirring occasionally, until the chicken is cooked through, 2–3 minutes. Add the udon noodles and cook, stirring, until warmed through, 2–3 minutes.

Transfer to a warmed serving dish, and serve.

22

MUSSELS FRA DIAVOLO WITH FENNEL, LEEKS & FREGOLA

serves 6

2 Tbsp olive oil

2 fennel bulbs, stalks and fronds removed, quartered and sliced

1 leek, chopped

4 cloves garlic, chopped

½ tsp red pepper flakes

Salt and freshly ground pepper

½ cup (4 fl oz/125 ml) red wine

1 can (28 oz/875 g) peeled whole tomatoes

3 cups (24 fl oz/750 ml) low-sodium chicken broth, plus more as needed

2 Tbsp minced fresh oregano

1 cup (8 oz/250 g) fregola

2 lb (1 kg) mussels, scrubbed and debearded

2 Tbsp chopped fresh flat-leaf parsley

Fra Diavolo translates to "brother devil" in Italian. In other words, spicy! Just ½ teaspoon red pepper flakes provides a serious punch of heat, which is known to help speed metabolism. Fregola, also derived from Italy, is round semolina pasta. These pearly grains build a hearty base in a fiery broth filled with vegetables and lean-protein mussels.

Warm the oil in a heavy pot over medium-high heat. Add the fennel, leek, and garlic and cook, stirring occasionally, until softened, about 5 minutes. Add the red pepper flakes and season with salt and pepper. Stir to combine and sauté until fragrant, about 1 more minute.

Add the wine and cook until the liquid is reduced by half, about 3 minutes. Add the whole tomatoes and, using a wooden spoon, break up the tomatoes in the saucepan. Add the broth and oregano and bring to a boil. Add the fregola and cook until the pasta is al dente, about 12 minutes, or according to package directions.

Add the mussels and cover the pot. Steam until the mussels open, 8–10 minutes.

Discard any mussels that haven't opened. Stir in more broth, if desired, and adjust the seasoning with salt and pepper. Sprinkle with the parsley, and serve.

23

Here we've taken the rich pork and excess breadcrumbs out of classic cassoulet, but preserved all the decadent French flavors. This healthier version is augmented with flavor-packed sun-dried tomatoes and meaty mushrooms.

VEGETARIAN CASSOULET

serves 6

1 cup (7 oz/220 g) dried small white beans

6 Tbsp (3 fl oz/90 ml) extra-virgin olive oil

1 *each* yellow onion and carrot, chopped

1 celery stalk, leaves reserved, chopped

4 cups (32 fl oz/1 l) low-sodium vegetable broth

1 sprig fresh thyme, plus 1 tsp minced

1 sprig fresh flat-leaf parsley

1 dried bay leaf

2 cloves garlic, minced, plus 10 garlic cloves

1 lb (500 g) red potatoes, unpeeled and cut into 2-inch (5-cm) chunks

1 red onion, cut into 1-inch (2.5-cm) chunks

Salt and freshly ground pepper

½ lb (500 g) portabello mushrooms, stems and gills removed, cut into large chunks

1 cup (8 fl oz/250 ml) dry white wine

½ cup (2½ oz/75 g) well-drained, oil-packed sun-dried tomatoes

Pick over the beans and discard any broken beans or grit. Rinse the beans well, place in a bowl, add water to cover by 2 inches (5 cm), and soak overnight.

In a saucepan over medium heat, warm 3 Tbsp of the olive oil. Add the onion, carrot, and celery and sauté until lightly browned, 5–7 minutes. Add the broth, raise the heat to high, and bring to a boil. Drain the beans and add them to the pan. Gather the thyme sprig, parsley sprig, bay leaf, and celery leaves into a bundle and tie securely with kitchen string. Add to the pan along with the minced garlic. Reduce the heat to low, cover, and simmer until the beans are tender, about 1½ hours. Discard the herb bundle.

Meanwhile, preheat the oven to 400°F (200°C). Lightly oil a large flameproof baking dish. In a large bowl, combine the potatoes, red onion, and the remaining 3 Tbsp olive oil. Toss to coat well. Spread in the prepared baking dish and sprinkle with 2 tsp salt.

Roast in the oven until lightly browned, about 45 minutes. Add the mushrooms and garlic cloves and continue to roast until the vegetables are browned, about 15 minutes longer. Remove from the oven, transfer the vegetables to a plate, and set aside. ⟫→

Place the baking dish on the stove top over medium heat. Pour in the wine and stir with a wooden spoon to scrape up the browned bits from the dish bottom. Continue to cook until the wine is almost evaporated, 5–7 minutes. Add the cooked beans and their liquid, the roasted vegetables, minced thyme, and sun-dried tomatoes. Season with salt and pepper. Continue to cook until the vegetables are tender, 15–20 minutes. Use a large spoon to serve.

24

The dense, sweet flesh of squash just begs to be roasted into syrupy, softened perfection. Other small winter squash, such as butternut squash, will also work well in this dish. Cut smaller squashes into cubes, roast them, and stir them into the cooked couscous. If roasting cubes instead of halves, decrease the roasting time by about 10 minutes.

ROASTED SQUASH WITH SPICED COUSCOUS

serves 4

2 acorn squash, each about 1¼ lb (750 g), halved and seeds removed

2 tsp olive oil

Salt and freshly ground pepper

1 cup (8 fl oz/250 ml) low-sodium vegetable broth

¾ cup (4½ oz/140 g) instant whole-wheat couscous

½ tsp ground cinnamon

¼ tsp ground ginger

½ Golden Delicious apple, cored and chopped

3 Tbsp sliced almonds, toasted

2 Tbsp dried currants

2 green onions, finely chopped

Preheat the oven to 400°F (200°C). Brush the squash halves with the oil and season with salt and pepper. Place the halves, cut side down, on a rimmed baking sheet. Roast until a thin knife easily pierces the squash, about 20 minutes.

Meanwhile, in a saucepan, bring the broth to a boil. Stir in the couscous, cinnamon, ginger, ½ tsp salt, and pepper to taste. Cover and set aside for 5 minutes.

Using a fork, stir the apple, almonds, currants, and green onions into the couscous. Spoon the couscous mixture into the roasted squash halves and serve.

25

PAN-SEARED HALIBUT WITH GRAPEFRUIT, PARSLEY & FENNEL SALAD

serves 4

Grapefruits are high in antioxidants. They add a pleasing tartness and fun pink color to any seafood dish. Halibut fillets cook quickly for an easy meal full of lean protein. Accompany this dish with a green salad.

4 pink or Ruby grapefruits

1 cup (1 oz/30 g) fresh flat-leaf parsley leaves

1 fennel bulb

4 halibut fillets, ½ lb (250 g) each, skin and pin bones removed

Salt and freshly ground pepper

1 Tbsp extra-virgin olive oil, plus more for drizzling

Cut a slice off both ends of each grapefruit so it will stand upright. Stand it on a cutting board and, using a large, sharp knife, cut away the peel and white pith by slicing from top to bottom, following the contour of the fruit. Using a small knife, cut along either side of each segment to free it from the membrane. As you work, let the segments and any juices fall into a bowl. Add the parsley to the bowl and stir gently.

Trim the fennel, peeling away any woody, fibrous outer layers and reserving the fronds. Using a mandoline or sharp knife, cut the fennel bulb into paper-thin slices. Add the fennel slices and fronds to the bowl.

Season the fillets with salt and pepper. In a heavy frying pan over medium-high heat, warm the 1 Tbsp olive oil. Add the fillets and cook until browned on one side, 3–4 minutes. Turn and cook until the fillets are opaque around the edges, about 3 minutes longer.

To serve, transfer fillets to individual plates. Spoon the grapefruit and fennel salad on top, and drizzle with a little olive oil.

26

SPLIT PEA SOUP WITH SPINACH

serves 4–6

A hearty, warming soup is the perfect thing for a cold winter evening. Split peas are an inexpensive staple to have on hand in the pantry and, unlike many dried legumes, they require no soaking before cooking. They also have a nutritional plus: dried peas contain about triple the protein found in fresh peas.

2 cups (14 oz/440 g) split peas

2 Tbsp olive oil

1 large yellow onion, chopped

2 carrots, peeled and chopped

1 dried bay leaf

6 cups (48 fl oz/1.5 l) low-sodium chicken or vegetable broth, plus more as needed

3 slices bacon (optional)

½ lb (250 g) spinach, tough stems removed, and finely chopped

Salt and freshly ground pepper

Pick over the split peas, discard any misshapen peas or stones, then rinse and drain well.

In a saucepan over medium heat, warm the oil. Add the onion and sauté until tender and translucent, about 10 minutes. Add the split peas, carrots, bay leaf, and 6 cups (48 fl oz/1.5 l) broth. Raise the heat to high and bring to a boil. Cover, reduce the heat to low, and simmer until the peas are very soft, about 45 minutes. If it becomes too thick, thin the soup with additional broth.

Meanwhile, if using the bacon, in a frying pan over medium heat, fry the bacon until crisp, about 5 minutes. Transfer to paper towels to drain. When cool, crumble.

When the soup is ready, discard the bay leaf. Add the spinach and simmer until it wilts, about 3 minutes. Remove from the heat and let cool slightly.

Working in batches, purée the soup base in a blender or food processor. Return to a clean saucepan and add broth as needed to thin it to the desired consistency. Place the pan over medium-high heat until warmed through. Season with salt and pepper.

Ladle the soup into warmed bowls, sprinkle with the crumbled bacon (if using), and serve.

27

Bright Asian seasonings such as ginger, lime, chile sauce, and fresh herbs help tofu and brown rice shine in this satisfying vegetarian meal. Peanuts add richness and crunch and sautéed shiitake mushrooms make delicious, meaty additions. The tofu can be marinated overnight for a bolder flavor.

SPICY TOFU, RICE & BROCCOLI SALAD

serves 4

Salt

1⅓ cups (9½ oz/295 g) brown basmati or jasmine rice

¼ cup (1 oz/30 g) peeled and thinly sliced fresh ginger

¼ cup (2 fl oz/60 ml) fresh lime juice

2 Tbsp low-sodium soy sauce

1 Tbsp Sriracha sauce

2 tsp Asian sesame oil

14–16 oz (440–500 g) firm tofu, drained, patted dry, and cut into ½-inch (12-mm) cubes

1½ lb (750 g) broccolini

½ cup (¾ oz/20 g) minced fresh cilantro

½ cup (¾ oz/20 g) minced fresh mint

½ cup (¾ oz/20 g) minced fresh basil

Dry roasted peanuts, coarsely chopped, for garnish

In a saucepan, bring 2 cups (16 fl oz/500 ml) salted water to a boil over high heat. Add the rice and return to a boil. Reduce the heat to low, cover, and cook for 45 minutes. Turn off the heat and let stand for 5 minutes. Fluff the rice with a fork, transfer to a large bowl, and let cool.

Meanwhile, in a food processor, combine the ginger, lime juice, soy sauce, Sriracha sauce, and sesame oil with 2 Tbsp water. Process until the ginger is finely minced. Transfer the mixture to a medium bowl. Mix in the tofu and let marinate.

Cut the broccolini into 2-inch (5-cm) pieces. In a steamer over boiling water, steam the broccoli until tender-crisp, about 3 minutes. Transfer the broccoli to a large bowl of cold water, then drain.

Add the broccolini to the rice. Stir in the marinated tofu, along with the marinade, cilantro, mint, and basil. Sprinkle with peanuts, and serve.

28

This play on classic mushroom and barley soup includes protein-rich chicken to keep you feeling fuller longer. The high levels of fiber found in barley are known to help lower cholesterol and aid digestion. Serve this soup alongside a green salad for a simple lunch or dinner.

MUSHROOM, CHICKEN & BARLEY SOUP

serves 4

½ cup (4 oz/125 g) pearl barley

1 chicken, about 3½ lb (1.75 kg), cut into 8 serving pieces and trimmed of excess fat

4 cups (32 fl oz/1 l) low-sodium chicken broth or water, or as needed

2 Tbsp olive oil

1 lb (500 g) assorted fresh, wild, or cultivated mushrooms, brushed clean, tough stems removed, and thickly sliced

Salt and freshly ground pepper

1 leek, white part only, chopped

1 shallot, minced

2 Tbsp chopped fresh flat-leaf parsley, plus extra for garnish

¼ cup (2 fl oz/60 ml) dry sherry or Madeira

Rinse the barley, place in a bowl, and add water to cover. Let soak for 2–3 hours.

Place the chicken pieces in a large pot. Add the broth to cover, and bring to a simmer over medium heat. Partially cover the pot and simmer gently, skimming occasionally, until the chicken juices run clear when the thickest part of a thigh is pierced knife, about 15 minutes. Using a slotted spoon, transfer the chicken to a dish and set aside to cool. Pour the broth into a large bowl.

Wipe out the pot, place over high heat, and add the oil. Add the mushrooms, season with salt and pepper, and cook, stirring often, until the mushrooms begin to brown and shrink, 5–7 minutes. (If necessary, cook the mushrooms in 2 batches; they should not be more than a single layer deep.) Add the leek, shallot, and 2 Tbsp parsley and sauté for 1 minute longer. Stir in the sherry and bring the mixture to a boil.

Drain the barley and add it to the pot along with the reserved broth. Bring to a boil, then reduce the heat to medium-low. Cover partially and simmer gently until the barley is tender, about 20 minutes.

Meanwhile, discard the skin and bones from the chicken and cut the meat into bite-size pieces. Add the chicken to the soup and heat through. Taste and adjust the seasonings. Ladle the soup into warmed bowls, garnish with parsley, and serve.

29

These tropical-inspired burgers use crab as a lean protein base. Crab is bursting in vitamin B-12, which helps form healthy blood cells. Bright mango and red onion provide a big dose of vitamins A and C. The salsa imparts a smoky flavor to the patties, thanks to a quick stint on the grill before dicing and mixing.

CRAB & JALAPEÑO BURGERS WITH GRILLED MANGO SALSA

serves 6

1 lb (500 g) crabmeat, picked over for cartilage

1 shallot, minced

1 jalapeño, seeds and ribs removed, then minced

¼ cup (⅓ oz/10 g) chopped fresh cilantro

¼ cup (2 fl oz/60 ml) olive-oil mayonnaise

¼ cup (¾ oz/20 g) whole-wheat panko bread crumbs

Salt and freshly ground pepper

FOR THE GRILLED MANGO SALSA

1 mango, ripe but still firm, peeled and pit removed to create two halves

¼ red onion, halved

1 tsp olive oil

1 Roma tomato, chopped

2 Tbsp chopped fresh cilantro

Juice of ½ lime

Salt and freshly ground pepper

Nonstick cooking spray

6 thin slices sourdough bread, toasted

In a large bowl, stir together the crab, shallot, jalapeño, cilantro, mayonnaise, and panko and stir to combine. Season with salt and pepper and form into 6 patties. Transfer to the refrigerator and chill for 30 minutes.

To make the salsa, warm a stove-top grill pan over high heat. Brush the mango and red onion with the oil and grill, turning once, until they develop grill marks and begin to soften, about 3–4 minutes per side. Chop the mango and onion into ¼-inch (6-mm) dice and transfer to a mixing bowl. Add the tomato, cilantro, and lime juice. Stir to mix and season with salt and pepper.

Warm a nonstick frying pan over medium-high and coat with nonstick cooking spray. Cook the patties, flipping once, until golden-brown and warmed through, about 4 minutes per side.

Place each crab patty on a slice of sourdough, top generously with the salsa, and serve.

30

This comforting soup comes together in a flash when you have leftover cooked chicken and rice on hand. If not, the meat from a store-bought rotisserie chicken and microwaveable brown rice will do just fine.

GREEK-STYLE CHICKEN SOUP

serves 4–6

1 Tbsp extra-virgin olive oil

3 carrots, sliced

1 small yellow onion, finely chopped

1 stalk celery, sliced

6 cups (48 fl oz/1.5 l) low-sodium chicken broth

2 cups (12 oz/375 g) shredded cooked chicken

2 cups (7 oz/220 g) cooked brown rice

3 Tbsp fresh lemon juice

2 Tbsp chopped fresh dill

Salt and freshly ground pepper

Warm a large saucepan over medium-high heat and add the oil. Add the carrots, onion, and celery and sauté until they have softened, about 2–3 minutes. Add the broth and bring to a boil. Reduce the heat to low and simmer until the vegetables are tender, about 20 minutes.

Add the chicken and rice and simmer until heated through, about 5 minutes. Stir in the lemon juice and dill. Season with salt and pepper. Ladle into warmed bowls and serve.

31

To save time, use a prepared curry paste to flavor the mild ingredients. Spoon the dish over brown rice and serve purchased chutney alongside.

CAULIFLOWER & TOFU CURRY

serves 4

1 Tbsp olive oil

1 large onion, finely chopped

14–16 oz (440–500 g) firm tofu, drained, patted dry, and cut into ¾-inch (2-cm) cubes

1 heaping Tbsp hot curry paste

1 head cauliflower, cut into ¾-inch (2-cm) florets

1 can (14.5 oz/455 g) diced tomatoes

In a large frying pan over medium-high heat, warm the oil. Add the onion and sauté until tender, about 5 minutes. Add the tofu and curry paste and stir to coat. Add the cauliflower, tomatoes and juices, and 1½ cups (12 fl oz/375 ml) water. Bring to a boil, cover, reduce the heat to medium-low, and simmer until the cauliflower is tender and the sauce thickens, about 20 minutes. Spoon into warmed shallow bowls, and serve.

Chilly winter days call for warming, wholesome meals. Reach for lean proteins, complex carbohydrates, and bright produce to compose meals that will both satisfy and nourish. Don't let dreary weather stop you from experimenting with vibrant colors and flavors. Novel sauces and garnishes bring new life to basics, like pairing vegetable rice paper rolls with creamy coconut milk-based peanut sauce and topping roasted salmon with a tropical avocado-grapefruit salsa.

february

POLENTA WITH CHEDDAR, CHARD & WILD MUSHROOMS

serves 4–6

This dish finds a near-perfect equilibrium of healthy and decadent. Creamy, cheesy polenta is balanced out with vitamin-rich mushrooms and chard. This comforting dish is warming on a cold winter's day.

Salt and freshly ground pepper

1½ cups (10½ oz/330 g) polenta

2 bunches chard, tough stems removed

1 fresh rosemary sprig, about 6 inches (15 cm) long

5 Tbsp (3 fl oz/80 ml) extra-virgin olive oil

1 Tbsp minced shallots

1 lb (500 g) assorted wild or cultivated mushrooms, cleaned and coarsely cut or left whole, depending on size

½ cup (2 oz/60 g) extra-sharp Cheddar cheese, shredded

In a large saucepan over high heat, bring 8 cups (64 fl oz/2 l) water and 1½ tsp salt to a boil. Add the polenta in a slow, steady stream, stirring constantly. Reduce the heat to low and cook, stirring often, until the polenta pulls away from the sides of the pan, 40–45 minutes.

Meanwhile, bring a large pot of water to a boil over high heat. Add the chard leaves and the rosemary sprig. Reduce the heat to medium and cook until the chard ribs are easily pierced with a fork, about 15 minutes. Drain well. Chop coarsely and squeeze dry.

In a frying pan over medium-high heat, warm 2 Tbsp of the olive oil. Add the shallots and mushrooms and cook until the mushrooms are tender, 8–10 minutes. Using a slotted spoon, transfer to a bowl. Reserve the juices.

When the polenta is ready, stir in the remaining 3 tablespoons olive oil, ¼ cup (1 oz/30 g) of the cheese, 1 tsp salt, and 1 tsp pepper and cook until the cheese has melted, 3–4 minutes longer. Return the frying pan to medium-high heat. Warm the juices, then add the chard and mushrooms and cook, stirring, until hot and well coated with the juices. Season with salt and pepper.

Spoon the polenta into a large warmed serving bowl, top with the chard and mushrooms, sprinkle with the remaining cheese, and serve.

CHOPPED CHICKEN SALAD

serves 4

A variety of textures, colors, and flavors define this tasty salad. Lean chicken meat is mixed into a bed of vegetables, and splashed with tangy vinaigrette. In place of the fennel or radishes, you can use cucumber, zucchini, or cauliflower. Omit the chicken to make a vegetarian salad or side dish.

FOR THE LEMON-TARRAGON VINAIGRETTE

6 Tbsp (3 fl oz/90 ml) fresh lemon juice

4 tsp minced fresh tarragon

4 tsp Dijon mustard

3 cloves garlic, minced

½ cup (4 fl oz/125 ml) extra-virgin olive oil

Salt and freshly ground pepper

4 skinless, boneless chicken breast halves

6 cups (48 fl oz/1.5 l) low-sodium chicken broth, or as needed

1 lb (500 g) hearts of romaine lettuce

½ small fennel bulb

24 small fresh mushrooms

20 radishes

4 small carrots

1 small head radicchio

1 small red onion

To make the vinaigrette, in a small bowl, whisk together the lemon juice, tarragon, mustard, and garlic. Gradually whisk in the oil and season with salt and pepper. Let stand for about 30 minutes before serving.

In a small saucepan over medium heat, combine the chicken breasts and broth as needed to cover. Bring to a simmer, adjust the heat to keep the broth just below a simmer, and cook, uncovered, until the chicken is just opaque throughout, about 10 minutes. Transfer the chicken to a cutting board; reserve the broth for another use. When the chicken is cool, cut it into bite-size pieces.

Chop the lettuce, fennel, mushrooms, radishes, carrots, radicchio, and onion into pieces approximately the same size as the chicken and put them in a large bowl. Add the chicken to the dressing and stir to coat, then pour the chicken and dressing over the vegetables. Toss well. Taste and adjust the seasoning, and serve.

LEMON CATFISH WITH SLAW

serves 8

8 catfish fillets, 6–8 oz (185–250 g) each, skinned

Salt and freshly ground pepper

¼ cup (2 fl oz/60 ml) *each* dry white wine and fresh lemon juice

Finely grated zest of 1 lemon

2 tsp Dijon mustard

1 tsp Asian sesame oil

⅓ cup (3 fl oz/80 ml) grapeseed oil

1 tsp sugar

2 Tbsp sesame seeds

½ *each* small head red and green cabbage, thinly sliced (about 2 cups/6 oz/185 g)

6 green onions, chopped

1 Tbsp peeled and minced fresh ginger

1 carrot, peeled and shredded

1 *each* red and yellow bell pepper, seeded and cut into 2-inch (5-cm) matchsticks

½ cup (⅔ oz/20 g) chopped fresh dill

16 thin lemon slices

Preheat the oven to 400°F (200°C). Pat the fillets dry and season with salt and pepper.

In a bowl, whisk together the wine, lemon juice and zest, and mustard. Slowly whisk in the oils, 1 tsp salt, 1 tsp pepper, and the sugar. Stir in the sesame seeds. In a large bowl, toss together the cabbages, green onions, ginger, carrot, bell peppers, and half of the chopped dill. Add half of the dressing and toss to coat.

Preheat the oven to 400°F (200°C). Cut 8 pieces of parchment paper, each about 12 by 18 inches (30 by 45 cm). Lay the pieces on a work surface and lightly oil the paper. Divide the slaw evenly among parchment pieces, placing it slightly off center. Place a fillet over each mound of slaw. Lay 2 lemon slices over each fillet. Drizzle the remaining dressing evenly over each portion, then top with the remaining chopped dill.

Fold the parchment in half over the fish by bringing the short sides together and folding them down to seal. Fold in the sides securely. Place the packets on a baking sheet and bake until the paper begins to brown and puff, 22–25 minutes. Place the packets on warmed individual plates. Carefully slit an X in each packet to let the steam escape, and serve.

Baking in parchment paper, also known as "en papillote" in French, is a great way to minimize cooking oils and clean-up. Perfect for dinner parties, individual parchment paper packets make portioning a cinch. Have guests open their own packets to reveal a fragrant lemony steam and a medley of bright vegetables and flaky fish inside.

KOREAN-STYLE NOODLES WITH MARINATED STEAK & KIMCHI

serves 4

3 Tbsp Asian sesame oil

1 Tbsp *each* low-sodium soy sauce and mirin

1 Tbsp brown sugar

1 tsp minced garlic

1 tsp Korean chile bean paste (such as gochujang) or Sriracha sauce

¼ cup toasted sesame seeds

12 oz (375 g) flank steak, sliced against the grain into thin strips

½ lb (250 g) bean thread noodles

2 Tbsp canola oil

½ lb (250 g) shiitake mushrooms, stemmed and thinly sliced

1 cup (3½ oz/105 g) thinly sliced onion

1 cup (5 oz/155 g) julienned carrot

¼ cup (1 oz/30 g) thinly sliced green onions

½ cup (2 oz/60 g) kimchi, coarsely chopped

In a baking dish, stir together the sesame oil, soy sauce, mirin, brown sugar, garlic, chile bean paste, and 2 Tbsp of the sesame seeds until the sugar dissolves. Set half of the mixture aside. Add the sliced steak to the remaining mixture. Cover and marinate in the refrigerator for at least 30 minutes and up to 4 hours. Remove the dish from the refrigerator 30 minutes before cooking.

Place the noodles in a heatproof bowl and cover with very hot tap water. Let the noodles soak until they become tender and opaque, about 10 minutes. Drain well.

Warm a wok over medium-high heat and add 1 Tbsp canola oil. Remove the meat from the marinade, letting any excess liquid drain off. Add the steak to the wok and stir-fry just until it begins to brown, 2–3 minutes. Transfer the steak to a plate. Warm the remaining 1 Tbsp canola oil in the wok, then add the mushrooms and onions. Stir-fry until the vegetables begin to soften, 2–3 minutes. Add the carrot and green onions and stir-fry until the onions are soft and lightly browned, 4–5 minutes. Stir in the noodles. Add the reserved sauce and the beef, stirring well to coat.

Transfer the noodles to a warm serving dish, garnish with the kimchi, and serve.

Kimchi is a Korean condiment of spicy, fermented cabbage. Raw cultured vegetables, such as those found in kimchi, are known to aid and cleanse digestive systems. This boldly flavored dish comes together quickly when the noodles and steak are made a day ahead of time. This dish also works well with a base of brown rice in place of the noodles.

5

Seafood and citrus make a foolproof combination. Cheery navel oranges (substitute half blood oranges, if available) add zing to sweet, plump scallops. A small amount of butter lends richness to the sauce without overdoing it.

PAN-SEARED SCALLOPS WITH ORANGE SAUCE

serves 4

2 navel oranges

Salt and freshly ground pepper

½ tsp ground cumin

1 lb (500 g) large sea scallops, side muscles removed

1 Tbsp olive oil

2 tsp sherry vinegar

1 Tbsp unsalted butter

2 tsp chopped fresh cilantro

Working with 1 orange at a time, cut a slice off both ends of each fruit so it will stand upright. Stand it on a cutting board, and using a large, sharp knife, cut away the peel and white pith by slicing from top to bottom, following the contour of the fruit. Cut the oranges into thin rounds and put in a bowl.

In a small dish, combine a pinch each of salt and pepper with the cumin. Sprinkle the scallops with the seasoning mixture.

In a frying pan over medium-high heat, warm the oil. Add the scallops and cook until browned on the bottom, 1–2 minutes. Turn over the scallops and cook until just firm to the touch and still a bit translucent in the center, 1–2 minutes. Transfer to a plate and cover to keep warm.

Add the juice from the bowl with the oranges and the vinegar to the pan and cook until reduced by half, 1–2 minutes. Add the orange slices and cook for 1 minute. Remove the pan from the heat and stir in the butter. Return the scallops and any juices to the pan and stir to coat with the sauce. Transfer the scallops to warmed plates and top with the sauce and orange slices. Sprinkle with cilantro, and serve.

6

Moroccan spices, such as cumin, turmeric, and cinnamon, help to make this a delicious and aromatic meal. Quinoa is a great gluten-free protein source and has a light and fluffy texture that's a nice counterpoint to tender root vegetables. Dried fruit and nuts are common in Moroccan-style dishes, and lend sweetness and crunch.

MOROCCAN-SPICED ROASTED VEGETABLES & QUINOA

serves 4–6

3 parsnips, cut into ½-inch (12-cm) pieces

2 carrots, cut into ½-inch (12-cm) pieces

6 Tbsp (3 fl oz/90 ml) olive oil

1 Tbsp ground cumin

2 tsp turmeric

1 tsp ground cinnamon

Salt and freshly ground pepper

2 cups (16 fl oz/500 ml) low-sodium chicken or vegetable broth

1 cup (8 oz/250 g) quinoa, rinsed

¼ cup (1½ oz/15 g) dried apricots, quartered

3 Tbsp slivered almonds, toasted

2 Tbsp chopped fresh flat-leaf parsley

Preheat the oven to 400°F (200°C). Toss the parsnips and carrots with 2 Tbsp of the oil, the cumin, turmeric, and cinnamon. Spread in a single layer on a baking sheet lined with parchment paper and season well with salt and pepper. Roast, stirring a couple of times, until the vegetables are very tender and caramelized, 35–40 minutes.

Bring the broth to a boil in a saucepan over high heat. Add the quinoa, cover, and reduce the heat to medium-low. Cook until all the broth is absorbed, about 12 minutes.

Transfer the quinoa to a large bowl and add the roasted vegetables, apricots, almonds, and parsley. Stir in the remaining 4 Tbsp (2 fl oz/60 ml) oil, season with salt and pepper, and serve.

7

This soup is a light interpretation of chicken tortilla soup. Spicy pickled jalapeños and fresh cilantro stand out as bright and flavorful highlights to the dish. Opt for whole-grain or blue corn tortilla chips for a healthy crunch.

CHICKEN & LIME SOUP WITH PICKLED JALAPEÑOS

serves 6

3 Tbsp olive oil

1 large yellow onion, chopped

2 Tbsp minced garlic

8 cups (64 fl oz/2 l) low-sodium chicken broth

1¼ lb (625 g) boneless, skinless chicken breasts

6 Tbsp (3 fl oz/90 ml) fresh lime juice

6 Tbsp (½ oz/15 g) chopped fresh cilantro

Salt and freshly ground pepper

¼ cup (2 oz/60 g) sliced pickled jalapeño chiles, or to taste

1 avocado, halved, pitted, and diced

Crumbled tortilla chips for garnish (optional)

In a large saucepan over medium heat, warm the oil. Add the onion and cook, stirring occasionally, until softened, about 10 minutes. Add the garlic and cook another 1–2 minutes. Add the broth, raise the heat to high, and bring to a boil.

Reduce the heat to medium-low and add the chicken. Simmer, partially covered, until cooked through, 10–12 minutes. Using a slotted spoon, transfer the chicken to a cutting board. Reduce the heat to low and keep the soup at a simmer.

When the chicken is cool enough to handle, shred it into bite-sized pieces. Stir the chicken into the soup along with the lime juice and cilantro. Season with salt and pepper, and simmer the soup until the chicken is heated through, about 5 minutes. Taste and adjust the seasoning if needed.

Ladle the soup into warmed bowls. Garnish with the jalapeños, diced avocado, and tortilla chips, if using, and serve.

8

Perfect for a dreary winter's day, the rainbow of colors in this salad are loaded with nutrients. Beets get their pigmentation from the same agents that are known to detoxify your system. Protect your hands from the stain of beets by wearing plastic gloves when peeling and cutting. This salad is nice sprinkled with a favorite herb, such as cilantro, basil, parsley, or thyme.

BEET, ORANGE & AVOCADO SALAD

serves 4

3 Tbsp extra-virgin olive oil

1 Tbsp sherry vinegar

1 large shallot, minced

1 clove garlic, minced

Salt and freshly ground pepper

3 red beets, about 1 lb (500 g) total weight

2 navel oranges or blood oranges, peel and pith removed and cut into segments

1 ripe but firm avocado

In a bowl, whisk together the oil, vinegar, shallot, garlic, and salt and pepper to make a vinaigrette.

Preheat the oven to 400°F (200°C). Put the beets in a baking dish and add water to a depth of ¼ inch (6 mm). Cover and bake until a knife pierces the beets easily, about 50 minutes. When cool enough to handle, peel and cut the beets into thin wedges. Place in a bowl and add enough of the vinaigrette to coat. Toss gently, then adjust the seasoning.

Put the orange segments in a bowl, add enough vinaigrette to coat, and toss gently. Halve, pit, peel, and thinly slice the avocado. Gently toss the avocado with the remaining vinaigrette. Arrange the avocado, orange, and beets on a platter or plates, and serve.

9

CLAMS WITH WHITE BEANS, FENNEL & BROCCOLI RABE

serves 2

1 fennel bulb, a few fronds reserved

½ tsp fennel seeds

1 Tbsp olive oil, plus more for drizzling

½ large red onion, finely chopped

¼–½ tsp red pepper flakes

½ cup (4 fl oz/125 ml) dry white wine

1 can (14.5 oz/455 g) cannellini beans, drained, juices reserved

1 bottle (8 fl oz/250 ml) clam juice

Large pinch of saffron threads

Freshly ground pepper

½ small bunch broccoli rabe, chopped

2 lb (1 kg) small clams, rinsed

Tender, sweet Manila clams take only minutes to cook. Here, they're augmented by fresh fennel, saffron, and red pepper flakes for a sophisticated dish. Serve with crusty whole-grain bread for a complete meal. This recipe can easily be doubled, but use a large Dutch oven to help the clams steam properly.

Cut the fennel bulb lengthwise into quarters, and then slice the quarters crosswise. In a mortar with a pestle or in a spice mill, coarsely grind the fennel seeds.

In a large nonstick frying pan over medium-high heat, warm the 1 Tbsp oil. Add the fennel slices, fennel seeds, onion, and pepper flakes and sauté until the fennel and onion start to soften, about 5 minutes. Add the wine and cook until it evaporates, about 1 minute. Add the drained beans, clam juice, saffron, and a generous amount of pepper, and simmer to blend the flavors, about 5 minutes. Add the broccoli rabe and simmer until it begins to wilt, about 1 minute. Add the clams. Stir in the reserved juice from the beans if the mixture is dry. Cover and steam until the clams open, about 5 minutes. Discard any clams that failed to open. Taste and adjust the seasoning.

Mince the reserved fennel fronds. Divide the clam mixture between 2 warmed deep bowls. Drizzle with oil, sprinkle with fennel fronds, and serve.

10

VEGETARIAN BORSCHT WITH HORSERADISH-DILL YOGURT

serves 6

Olive oil

6 red beets with greens attached, about 2 lb (1 kg) total weight

6 cups (48 fl oz/1.5 l) low-sodium vegetable broth

¼ cup (2 fl oz/60 ml) tomato sauce

2 celery stalks, sliced

2 carrots, grated

1 yellow onion, chopped

1 small russet potato, peeled and diced

½ cup (4 fl oz/125 ml) plain Greek yogurt

1 Tbsp minced fresh dill

1 tsp prepared horseradish

Salt and freshly ground pepper

Although borscht is often served chilled, this version is at its best piping hot for lunch or dinner on a chilly day. Roasting the beets brings out their natural sweetness, and the beet greens add an extra measure of flavor, texture, and nutrients.

Preheat the oven to 400°F (200°C). Lightly oil a baking sheet.

Trim the beet greens and set aside. Quarter the beets lengthwise and place them on the prepared baking sheet. Roast until softened and lightly browned, 15–20 minutes. Remove from the oven and let cool.

Peel the beets and cut into bite-sized chunks. Thinly slice enough beet greens to measure 1 cup (3 oz/90 g). Set aside.

In a saucepan over medium heat, combine the broth, tomato sauce, celery, carrots, onion, and potato. Bring to a boil, reduce the heat to low, and simmer, uncovered, until the vegetables are tender, about 20 minutes. Add the beets and beet greens and simmer until the beets are tender and the greens are wilted, about 10 minutes longer.

Meanwhile, in a small bowl, stir together the yogurt, dill, and horseradish until blended.

Season the soup with salt and pepper. Ladle the soup into warmed bowls, top each with a spoonful of the yogurt mixture, and serve.

11

Barley is rich in cholesterol-lowering soluble fiber. Here it stars as the base for a hearty greens-and-grains vegetarian dish. For extra protein and flavor, stir in kidney beans or chickpeas just before serving.

BARLEY WITH KALE & LEMON

serves 2–4

Salt

½ cup (3½ oz/105 g) pearl barley

1 bunch (about 1 lb/500 g) lacinato kale

2 Tbsp extra-virgin olive oil

1 small yellow onion, finely chopped

4 cloves garlic, chopped

¼ tsp red pepper flakes

½ tsp grated lemon zest

1–2 Tbsp fresh lemon juice

Fill a large saucepan halfway with salted water and bring to a boil over high heat. Add the barley and cook until tender, about 45 minutes. Drain and set aside.

Meanwhile, using a sharp knife, remove the center ribs from the kale leaves and discard. Stack the leaves, roll them into a cylinder, and cut crosswise into thin strips.

In a large, heavy frying pan over medium-high heat, warm the oil. Add the onion and sauté until golden-brown, about 6 minutes. Add the garlic and sauté until fragrant, about 1 minute. Reduce the heat to medium, add the kale, and sprinkle with the red pepper flakes. Sauté until the kale is tender and wilted, about 7 minutes.

Stir in the lemon zest and season with salt, then add the lemon juice to taste. Transfer to a warmed serving dish and serve.

12

Tangy grapefruit combined with silky avocado, sharp red onion, and bright fresh cilantro makes a lively topping for wild Alaskan king salmon—a great sustainable fish choice. Salmon and avocados are full of omega-3 fatty acids—a good type of fat. This recipe can be doubled for a family meal or dinner party and served with rice pilaf and sautéed cabbage.

ROASTED SALMON WITH AVOCADO-GRAPEFRUIT SALSA

serves 2

¾ lb (375 g) wild salmon fillet, about 1½-inch (4-cm) thick

Olive oil, for brushing

Salt and freshly ground pepper

Ancho chile powder

1 large grapefruit

1 small, firm but ripe avocado, pitted, peeled, and cubed

½ large jalapeño chile, seeded and minced

3 Tbsp red onion, minced

2 Tbsp fresh cilantro, minced

1 Tbsp fresh lime juice

Preheat the oven to 375°F (190°C). Place the fish in a small baking pan and brush on both sides with oil. Season lightly with salt, pepper, and chile powder. Roast until the salmon is almost opaque in the center, about 18 minutes.

Meanwhile, using a sharp knife, cut off the peel and all of the white pith from the grapefruit. Working over a medium bowl, use a paring knife to cut between the membranes to release the grapefruit segments into the bowl. Squeeze the juice from the membranes into the bowl. Remove the grapefruit segments from the bowl and cut crosswise into ½-inch (12-mm) pieces; return to the bowl. Gently stir in the avocado, jalapeño, onion, cilantro, and lime juice. Season the salsa with salt and pepper.

Cut the fish in half and divide between 2 warmed plates. Spoon the salsa over the top, and serve.

13

You'll want to make extras of this creamy peanut sauce to use as dip for leftover raw vegetables. Luscious coconut milk and rich peanut butter come together to make a condiment that seems decadent, but is actually nutritious. Peanuts and coconuts are full of healthy fats that turn light vegetable rolls into a satisfying dish.

VEGETABLE RICE PAPER ROLLS WITH PEANUT SAUCE

makes 24 rolls; serves 6

FOR THE PEANUT SAUCE

½ cup (4 fl oz/125 ml) coconut milk

½ cup (5 oz/155 g) peanut butter

1 green onion, minced

3-inch (7.5-cm) piece lemongrass, minced

2 cloves garlic, minced

Juice of ½ lime

1 Tbsp low-sodium soy sauce

1 tsp *each* curry powder and ground coriander

½ tsp ground cumin

1 tsp Sriracha sauce, or to taste

FOR THE ROLLS

½ lb (250 g) dried rice stick noodles

3 Tbsp peanut oil

1 clove garlic, minced

½ tsp Asian sesame oil

½ lb (250 g) Chinese broccoli or broccoli rabe, trimmed and coarsely chopped

1 carrot, coarsely grated

½ cup (1 oz/30 g) mung bean sprouts

24 rice paper rounds, 6 inches (15 cm) in diameter

Fresh mint and cilantro leaves

To make the sauce, in a saucepan over medium heat, combine the coconut milk, peanut butter, green onion, lemongrass, garlic, lime juice, soy sauce, curry powder, coriander, and cumin and stir until well blended. Transfer to a blender or food processor and purée until smooth, thinning with water if necessary. Pour into a bowl and stir in the Sriracha sauce. Set aside.

To make the rolls, in a heatproof bowl, soak the noodles in hot water to cover for 15 minutes. Drain the noodles and cut into 2-inch (5-cm) lengths. Set aside.

In a wok over medium heat, warm the peanut oil. Add the garlic and stir-fry until lightly golden, about 2 minutes. Add the sesame oil, broccoli, and carrot and stir-fry until softened, 4–5 minutes. Add the noodles and stir-fry until the noodles are hot, 2–3 minutes. Stir in the sprouts and set aside. »→

Working with 1 rice paper round at a time, place the round on a work surface and brush liberally with water. Let stand for a minute or two until pliable. Transfer to a flat plate and place a heaping tablespoon of filling in the center. Top with a few mint and cilantro leaves. Turn up two sides and roll into a cylinder. Continue with the remaining rice paper rounds.

Arrange the rolls on a platter or plates and serve with the peanut sauce for dipping.

14

Rich in beta-carotene and packed with vitamins A and C, broccoli rabe is a healthy powerhouse. Creamy protein-packed fried eggs, grilled whole-grain bread, and a punch of metabolism-boosting red pepper flakes complete this simple but satisfying meal. This dish is perfect for breakfast, a light lunch, or as a hearty first course.

SPICY BROCCOLI RABE BRUSCHETTA WITH FRIED EGGS

serves 4

Salt and freshly ground pepper

1 bunch broccoli rabe, trimmed

3 Tbsp olive oil

4 slices crusty whole-grain Italian-style bread (about 1-inch/2.5-cm slices)

1 clove garlic, halved lengthwise

½ tsp red pepper flakes

1 Tbsp fresh lemon juice

4 large eggs

Bring a large saucepan of water to a boil over medium-high heat. Add a big pinch of salt and the broccoli rabe. Cook until tender, about 3 minutes. Drain and rinse under cold water. Lay flat on paper towels to dry.

Warm a stove-top grill pan over high heat. Using 1 Tbsp of the oil, brush the bread on both sides. Grill the bread until golden, about 4 minutes per side. Rub each slice with the cut side of a garlic clove. Transfer to a platter.

In a nonstick frying pan over medium-high heat, warm 1 Tbsp of the oil. Add the pepper flakes and cook just until fragrant, about 1 minute. Add the broccoli rabe and stir to coat with oil. Season with salt and pepper, and stir in the lemon juice. Divide the broccoli rabe evenly over the bread slices. In the same frying pan, warm the remaining 1 Tbsp oil. Add the eggs and fry until the whites are set but the yolks are still runny, 5–6 minutes. Lay the fried eggs on top of the broccoli rabe. Season with salt and pepper, and serve.

SAUTÉED SOLE WITH FENNEL & LEMON COMPOTE

serves 4

3 Tbsp olive oil

2 large fennel bulbs, fronds reserved, trimmed, cored, and cut into thin slices

Salt and freshly ground pepper

¼ cup (2 fl oz/60 ml) dry white wine

Finely grated zest of 1 lemon and 1 Tbsp lemon juice

2 tsp sugar

⅓ cup (3 fl oz/80 ml) grapeseed oil

1 egg

2 or 3 drops hot red-pepper sauce

1¾ cups (2½ oz/75 g) whole-wheat panko bread crumbs

2 Tbsp all-purpose flour

4 fillets of sole, about 6 oz (185 g) each

2 Tbsp chopped fresh flat-leaf parsley

Low-fat sole forms a delicious crust when seared at high temperatures. It's perfect for cooking in grapeseed oil, which is full of essential fatty acids and retains its nutritional value at a high smoke point. Whole-wheat panko makes a crisp crust and is a more healthful choice for coating fish than white flour.

In a saucepan over medium heat, warm the olive oil. Add the fennel slices and ½ tsp salt and sauté until lightly browned, 3–4 minutes. Stir in the wine, lemon zest and juice, and sugar. Cover the pan, reduce the heat to low, and cook until the fennel is very soft, 5–6 minutes. Keep warm.

Warm a very large sauté pan over medium-high heat and add the grapeseed oil. Meanwhile, in a large, shallow dish, whisk together the egg, pepper sauce, ¼ tsp salt, and a few grinds of pepper. Add the panko and flour to separate shallow dishes. Lightly flour a fish fillet on both sides, dip it into the egg mixture, and then into the panko, coating both sides evenly. Gently place the breaded fillet into the hot oil and, working quickly, repeat with the remaining fillets. Sauté the fillets until nicely browned on the first side, about 3 minutes. Turn the fillets and sauté until the second side is browned and the fish is opaque throughout, about 2 minutes longer.

Transfer the fillets to warmed plates and spoon the compote alongside. Sprinkle with the parsley, and serve.

LEG OF LAMB WITH ROASTED FENNEL & PAN SAUCE

serves 4

2 Tbsp *each* minced shallot, minced fresh thyme, and grated orange zest

2¼ tsp fennel seeds, crushed

1¼ lb (625 g) boneless leg of lamb, trimmed

Salt and freshly ground pepper

1 Tbsp olive oil, plus more for brushing

1 large fennel bulb, trimmed, cored, and cut lengthwise into wedges about ¼-inch (6-mm) thick

1 large red onion, cut lengthwise into thin wedges

⅓ cup (3 fl oz/80 ml) dry vermouth

⅓ cup (3 fl oz/80 ml) low-sodium chicken broth

This juicy lamb comes together quickly when the seasoning mixture is made a day ahead of time. Spread half of the seasoning on the lamb, refrigerate it for up to 1 day, and then pop it in the oven when you're ready to cook. Roasted fingerling potatoes, tossed with olive oil and rosemary, make an appealing side dish.

Preheat the broiler. In a small bowl, mix together the shallot, thyme, orange zest, and fennel seeds. Place the lamb on a broiler pan and season it with salt and a generous amount of pepper. Rub half the shallot mixture all over the lamb, and then brush it with oil.

Broil the lamb until a thermometer inserted in the thickest part registers 125°–130°F (52°–54°C) for medium-rare, about 8 minutes on each side. Transfer the lamb to a warmed platter and tent loosely with foil.

In a large bowl, combine the fennel and onion. Add the 1 Tbsp oil and toss to coat. Set aside 1 Tbsp of the shallot mixture for the sauce; add the remaining mixture to the vegetables and toss to coat. Season with salt and pepper. Brush a large, heavy baking sheet with oil; transfer the vegetables to the sheet and arrange in a single layer. Broil the vegetables until they start to brown, about 7–8 minutes, stirring halfway through.

De-fat the juices in the broiler pan. Set the pan on the stove top over medium heat. Add the vermouth and bring to a boil, stirring up the browned bits on the pan bottom. Boil until syrupy, about 3 minutes. Add the broth and boil until it thickens slightly, about 2 minutes. Mix in the reserved shallot mixture and any lamb juices from the platter. Taste and adjust the seasoning.

Slice the meat thinly and serve with the vegetables and sauce.

17

TURKEY BURGERS WITH RADICCHIO SLAW

serves 4

3 Tbsp olive oil mayonnaise

1½ Tbsp whole-grain Dijon mustard

3 Tbsp capers, rinsed and minced

1¼ lb (625 g) ground turkey

1 Tbsp fresh thyme, minced

4 Tbsp (2 fl oz/60 ml) extra-virgin olive oil, plus more for brushing

1 large shallot, minced

Salt and freshly ground pepper

1 head radicchio, cut into quarters, then thinly sliced

1½ Tbsp balsamic vinegar

4 whole-grain rolls, split

The wine-red color and bitter flavor in leafy radicchio come from its high density of antioxidants. Here radicchio makes a fast and fresh slaw topping. Be sure to make extra of this creamy sauce to use as a dip for fresh vegetables served on the side. Any kind of turkey meat will work here, but lean meat is the healthiest option.

In a small bowl, combine the mayonnaise, mustard, and 1½ Tbsp capers. Refrigerate until ready to serve.

In a bowl, combine the turkey, thyme, and remaining 1½ Tbsp capers. In a small frying pan over medium heat, warm 1 Tbsp of the oil. Add the shallot and sauté until tender, about 4 minutes. Add to the turkey along with ¾ tsp salt and a generous amount of pepper. Mix gently to combine. Form the mixture into 4 patties, each about ½-inch (12-mm) thick. Brush the cut surface of the rolls with oil, and sprinkle with pepper.

Preheat the broiler. Heat a large frying pan over medium heat; brush with oil. Add the patties and cook until cooked through, about 5 minutes on each side.

Meanwhile, in another bowl, toss the radicchio with the vinegar and the remaining 3 Tbsp oil. Season to taste with salt and pepper.

Place the rolls, cut side up, on a rimmed baking sheet. Broil until golden-brown, about 4 minutes.

To serve, divide the roll bottoms among 4 warmed plates. Top them with the patties, sauce, and slaw, and cover with the roll tops. Spoon the remaining slaw alongside the burgers, and serve.

18

CAULIFLOWER STEAKS WITH CAPER-ANCHOVY-GARLIC SAUCE

serves 4

1 head cauliflower, very bottom of the head trimmed but stem left intact

4 Tbsp (2 fl oz/60 ml) olive oil

Salt and freshly ground pepper

4 cloves garlic, chopped

3 anchovies packed in oil, chopped

¼ cup (2 oz/60 g) capers, drained

1 lemon, halved

This dish makes a satisfying vegetable-based main course or a fresh accompaniment to grilled or roasted meat. Brain-fueling cauliflower, packed with B vitamins, is a smart choice in this simple yet elegant dish. Don't worry if you have some extra pieces of cauliflower that don't form a whole steak. They look fantastic on the plate next to the rest of the steaks.

Preheat the oven to 400°F (200°C).

Place the cauliflower on a cutting board, stem side down, and cut into ¾-inch (2-cm) slices. Place the cauliflower slices on a baking sheet lined with parchment paper. Using 1 Tbsp of the oil, brush the steaks and season them lightly with salt and pepper.

In a small frying pan over low heat, warm the remaining 3 Tbsp olive oil. Add the garlic, anchovies, and capers and sauté until the garlic is soft and the anchovies begin to dissolve, about 10 minutes.

Spoon the anchovy sauce on top of the cauliflower. Roast the cauliflower until it is caramelized and soft, about 20 minutes. Squeeze ½ the lemon on top.

Using a spatula, carefully transfer the cauliflower slices to a platter and serve with the remaining ½ lemon, cut into wedges for squeezing.

19

This lightened version of a classic Italian comfort food uses heart-healthy olive oil in place of butter and leaves out the flour coating. A variety of fresh and dried Italian herbs bring authentic flavors to this aromatic stew. Serve over soft polenta (page 89), which you can make while the chicken is simmering.

CHICKEN CACCIATORE

serves 4

1 chicken, about 3½ lb (1.75 kg), cut into 8 serving pieces

Salt and freshly ground pepper

3 Tbsp olive oil

1 yellow onion, chopped

2 cloves garlic, minced

10 oz (315 g) white mushrooms, quartered

1 green bell pepper, seeded and chopped

1 Tbsp tomato paste

½ cup (4 fl oz/125 ml) dry red wine

1 can (28 oz/875 g) crushed tomatoes

1 tsp dried oregano

1 fresh rosemary sprig, 3 inches (7.5 cm) long

1 dried bay leaf

Pat the chicken pieces dry with paper towels and sprinkle with salt and pepper. In a frying pan over medium-high heat, warm 2 Tbsp of the oil. Add the chicken pieces and cook, turning as needed, until browned on all sides, about 8 minutes total. Transfer to a plate.

Add the remaining 1 Tbsp oil to the pan and warm over medium-high heat. Add the onion and sauté until it begins to soften, about 3 minutes. Add the garlic, mushrooms, and bell pepper and sauté until softened, about 3 minutes. Add the tomato paste and stir to dissolve and coat the vegetables. Pour in the wine, bring to a boil, and stir, using a wooden spoon to scrape up the browned bits from the pan bottom. Add the tomatoes with their juice, oregano, rosemary, and bay leaf and return to a boil. Return the chicken to the pan, along with any accumulated juices, and spoon the sauce over it. Reduce the heat to medium-low, cover, and cook, stirring and turning the chicken pieces occasionally, until the chicken is tender when pierced with a sharp knife, 18–20 minutes longer.

Transfer the chicken to a warmed platter and cover loosely with foil. Continue to cook the sauce over medium-high heat until thickened, about 5 minutes.

Remove and discard the rosemary and bay leaf from the sauce and season with salt and pepper. Pour the sauce over the chicken, and serve.

20

Serve this dish with a green goddess dressing. Finely chop ½ cup (½ oz/15 g) fresh flat-leaf parsley, 2 Tbsp dill, 1 Tbsp mint, and 1 green onion in a food processor. Add ½ cup (4 fl oz/ 125 ml) low-fat buttermilk, ½ cup (4 oz/125 g) low-fat plain yogurt, 1 Tbsp olive oil, and salt to taste and process until smooth.

GRILLED WINTER VEGETABLES WITH ROSEMARY

serves 6–8

Salt and freshly ground pepper

6 *each* carrots and parsnips, peeled and halved lengthwise

2 rutabagas, peeled and sliced crosswise ½ inch (12 mm) thick

1 butternut squash, peeled, halved lengthwise, seeded, and cut into large chunks

Olive oil for brushing

1 tsp dried rosemary, crumbled

Fill a large pot three-fourths full of salted water and bring to a rapid boil. Add the carrots, parsnips, rutabagas, and squash and cook until just tender, 7–10 minutes. Using a slotted spoon, lift out the vegetables, draining well. Warm a stove-top grill pan over medium-high heat. Brush the vegetables generously with oil, and sprinkle with the rosemary. Grill the vegetables, turning as needed, until tender, 5–7 minutes for the carrots and parsnips and about 12 minutes for the rutabagas and butternut squash. Transfer to a platter, season with salt and pepper, and serve.

21

When broken into with a fork, the egg yolks run onto the greens and mingle with the dressing to make a creamy sauce.

BITTER GREENS SALAD WITH POACHED EGGS

serves 2

¼ cup (2 fl oz/60 ml) extra-virgin olive oil

3 Tbsp red wine vinegar

½ shallot, minced

Salt and freshly ground pepper

2 cups (2 oz/60 g) *each* baby dandelion greens and torn frisée

4 eggs, poached (see page 89)

In a large bowl, stir together the oil, vinegar, shallot, ½ tsp salt, and ½ tsp pepper to make a vinaigrette. Add the greens and toss well. Divide evenly among salad plates.

Poach the eggs as directed. Using a slotted spoon, place 1 egg on top of each salad. Season with salt and pepper, and serve.

SPAGHETTI WITH SHRIMP, FENNEL, TOMATOES & OLIVES

serves 2

Salt and freshly ground black pepper

1½ Tbsp olive oil

½ tsp fennel seeds

1 large fennel bulb, cored and thinly sliced lengthwise, fronds chopped and reserved

1 yellow onion, halved and thinly sliced

Red pepper flakes

1 can (14.28 oz/448 g) Italian tomatoes, preferably San Marzano

¼ cup (1 oz/30 g) pitted Kalamata olives, quartered lengthwise

3 Tbsp dry white wine

7–8 oz (220–250 g) spaghetti, preferably multigrain

½ lb (250 g) shrimp, peeled and deveined

Slightly licorice-tasting, crunchy fennel is chock-full of essential vitamins and minerals. Multigrain spaghetti and low-fat shrimp make this dish light and satisfying, while simmered olives and tomatoes envelop the dish in a savory sauce. This recipe can be doubled to feed a group.

Bring a large pot three-fourths full of salted water to a boil.

Meanwhile, in a large frying pan over medium-high heat, warm the oil. Add the fennel seeds and stir until fragrant, about 10 seconds. Add the fennel bulb, onion, and a large pinch of red pepper flakes. Season with salt and black pepper. Sauté, stirring frequently, until the fennel and onion are tender and browning on the edges, about 10 minutes. Add the tomatoes with their juices, the olives, and wine. Simmer, breaking up the tomatoes with a wooden spoon, until the sauce thickens, about 5 minutes.

While the tomatoes are simmering, add the pasta to the boiling water, stir well, and cook until al dente, about 11 minutes.

After the tomatoes have simmered for 5 minutes, add the shrimp to the frying pan and simmer until they are just opaque at the center, about 5 minutes; do not overcook.

Drain the pasta, add to the sauce, and stir to coat the pasta. Taste and adjust the seasonings. Transfer to a large warmed bowl, sprinkle with the fennel fronds, and serve.

LENTIL & ESCAROLE SOUP

serves 6

¼ cup (2 fl oz/60 ml) olive oil

1 yellow onion, chopped

2 *each* celery stalks and carrots, chopped

2 cloves garlic, chopped

1 can (14.5 oz/455 g) diced tomatoes

2¼ cups (1 lb/500 g) green lentils

8 cups (64 fl oz/2 l) low-sodium chicken or beef broth

1 small head escarole, chopped

Salt and freshly ground pepper

½ cup (2 oz/60 g) grated Parmesan cheese

Escarole is a green vegetble with robust, curly leaves that have a slightly bitter taste. Wilted in a hearty lentil soup, escarole brings texture and new flavors to an old favorite. This soup satisfies hunger with protein and fiber-filled lentils.

In a large saucepan over medium heat, warm the olive oil. Add the onion, celery, and carrots and sauté until golden, about 1 minute. Add the garlic and cook until fragrant, about 1 minute. Add the tomatoes with their juice, bring to a simmer, and cook, uncovered, for 10 minutes.

Pick over the lentils, discarding any stones or misshapen lentils. Rinse well and add to the saucepan. Stir well, add the broth, and bring to a simmer over medium heat. Reduce the heat to low and simmer until the lentils are partially softened, about 30 minutes. Add the escarole, season with salt and pepper, and cook until the lentils are tender, about 30 minutes longer.

Ladle the soup into warmed soup bowls, sprinkle with the cheese, and serve.

24

WHOLE-WHEAT PENNE WITH BRAISED GARLIC & RADICCHIO

serves 4

Pungent braised garlic brings a depth of flavor and nutrients to this simple pasta dish. Garlic is known to have anti-inflammatory, antibacterial, and antimicrobial powers, making it a nutritional triple-threat.

20 cloves garlic

Salt and freshly ground pepper

¼ cup (2 fl oz/60 ml) extra-virgin olive oil, plus extra for drizzling

4 heads Treviso radicchio, cored and thinly sliced

Leaves from 2 or 3 small fresh rosemary sprigs, minced

Splash of balsamic vinegar

1 lb (500 g) whole-wheat penne

½ cup (2½ oz/75 g) pine nuts, lightly toasted

½ cup (2 oz/60 g) grated pecorino romano cheese

Handful of fresh flat-leaf parsley leaves, coarsely chopped

In a small saucepan over high heat, combine the garlic cloves with water to cover and bring to a boil. Reduce the heat to medium and simmer until the cloves are soft enough to pierce easily with a knife, about 5 minutes. Drain well.

Bring a large pot of salted water to a boil.

Meanwhile, in a large frying pan or flameproof baking dish over medium heat, warm the ¼ cup (2 fl oz/60 ml) olive oil. Add the garlic cloves and sauté until lightly golden, 1–2 minutes. Add the radicchio, season with salt and pepper to taste, and sauté until the radicchio just starts to wilt, 3–4 minutes. Add a splash of water to the pan and continue cooking until the radicchio is tender, about 4 minutes. There should be some liquid left in the pan. Add the rosemary and balsamic vinegar and cook for 1 minute to blend the flavors.

Add the penne to the boiling water and cook until al dente, 10–12 minutes. Drain. Add the pasta to the frying pan with the vegetables and toss over low heat to mix well.

Pour the pasta mixture into a warmed large, shallow bowl. Add the pine nuts, cheese, parsley, and a drizzle of olive oil. Toss to melt the cheese and to mix all the ingredients, and serve.

25

CHOPPED CHARD SALAD WITH GRAPEFRUIT VINAIGRETTE

serves 4–6

This colorful salad is as healthy as it is delicious. Fiber-rich chard lends a leafy crunch, while avocados provide a smooth textural contrast and are full of healthy fats. Crisp apples and tart grapefruit add a subtle sweetness without overpowering the simple freshness of the salad.

2 bunches chard, chopped

3 carrots, shredded

2 avocados, pitted, peeled, and thinly sliced

1 apple, cored and thinly sliced

3 Tbsp slivered almonds, toasted

FOR THE GRAPEFRUIT VINAIGRETTE

1 shallot, minced

5 Tbsp (3 fl oz/80 ml) fresh grapefruit juice

2 Tbsp extra-virgin olive oil

Salt and freshly ground pepper

In a bowl, toss the chard, carrots, avocados, apple, and almonds to combine.

To make the vinaigrette, place the shallot and the grapefruit juice in a small bowl. Whisk in the extra-virgin olive oil and season to taste with salt and pepper.

Add the vinaigrette to the salad and toss to combine. Season with salt and pepper, and serve.

26

Calorie-laden pizza gets a makeover in this healthy rendition. Part-skim mozzarella keeps the topping creamy, but low in fat. Nutty niçoise olives develop a pleasing leathery texture in the oven. The pizza is perfect for lunch or dinner, but, cut into small squares, it also makes a tempting shared snack or appetizer.

BROCCOLI RABE & OLIVE PIZZA

serves 2–3

1 lb (500 g) purchased whole-wheat pizza dough, at room temperature

2 Tbsp extra-virgin olive oil

1 large clove garlic, minced

¼ tsp red pepper flakes

Pinch of salt

1 bunch broccoli rabe, about ¾ lb (375 g), thick stems removed

Flour and cornmeal, for dusting

½ lb (250 g) part-skim mozzarella cheese, coarsely shredded

¼ cup (2 oz/60 g) pitted niçoise olives

Position a rack in the bottom of the oven. Place a baking stone on the rack. Preheat the oven to 550°F (290°C), or the highest setting, for at least 45 minutes. Punch the dough down and turn it out onto a work surface. Shape it into a ball. Cover with a clean kitchen towel and let rest for 30 minutes.

In a small bowl, combine the oil, garlic, red pepper flakes, and salt. Let stand for 30 minutes to marry the flavors.

Bring a large pot three-fourths full of salted water to a boil over high heat. Add the broccoli rabe and cook until tender, 2–3 minutes. Drain and cool under running cold water. Gently squeeze out the excess water. Roughly chop the broccoli rabe.

To assemble the pizza, lightly flour a work surface. Roll out the dough into a round 13–14 inches (33–35 cm) in diameter. Generously dust a pizza peel or rimless baking sheet with cornmeal and transfer the dough round to it. Working quickly, spread the cheese evenly over the dough, leaving a ¾-inch (2-cm) rim uncovered. Top evenly with the broccoli rabe and the olives. Brush the rim with some of the seasoned oil, then drizzle more oil evenly over the pizza.

Immediately slide the pizza from the peel onto the baking stone. Bake until the crust is crisp and browned, about 8 minutes. Remove from the oven. Brush the rim of the crust with any remaining oil, and serve.

27

Green papaya is known to be a natural immune system booster. Here it's dressed in a bold Asian dressing. Add your favorite grilled protein, such as shrimp, tofu, or chicken, to make this dish a meal.

GREEN PAPAYA SALAD

serves 4–6

1½ lb (750 g) green papayas (about 2), peeled, seeded, and shredded

1 carrot, peeled and shredded

5 shallots, 4 thinly sliced and 1 chopped

1 red chile, seeded and sliced into thin rings

2 cloves garlic, chopped

1 tsp sugar

¼ tsp salt

¼ cup (2 fl oz/60 ml) rice vinegar

3 Tbsp *each* Asian fish sauce and fresh lime juice

2 tsp Sriracha sauce

3 Tbsp peanut oil

2 Tbsp chopped fresh cilantro leaves

In a large bowl, combine the papayas, carrot, sliced shallots, and chile, and toss to mix. In a mini food processor, process the garlic, chopped shallot, sugar, and salt until a paste forms. Transfer the paste to a bowl and whisk in the vinegar, fish sauce, lime juice, and Sriracha. Whisk in the oil. Pour the dressing over the papaya mixture, add the cilantro, and toss well. Let stand for 1 hour, and serve.

28

Stracciatella means "little rag" in Italian, which describes the shreds of egg and cheese in this favorite Roman soup. The deep green strips of spinach add a boost of color and nutrients.

SPINACH STRACCIATELLA

serves 4–6

6 cups (48 fl oz/1.5 l) low-sodium chicken broth

4 large eggs

¼ cup (1 oz/30 g) grated Parmesan cheese

1 cup (2 oz/60 g) packed, finely shredded spinach leaves

In a saucepan, bring the broth to a boil over high heat. Meanwhile, in a bowl, lightly beat the eggs and then stir in the cheese until well blended.

Reduce the heat so the broth is briskly simmering. While stirring the broth constantly and steadily, drizzle in the egg mixture to form long strands. Stir in the spinach and simmer for 2–3 minutes. Ladle into warmed bowls, and serve.

Signs of spring begin to emerge at the market, where suddenly, bright, fresh produce is displayed in abundance. Snow peas and asparagus make their debut, and can be supplemented in nearly any stir-fry or salad for added nutrients. Celebrate the beginning of the season with healthy dishes that highlight spring's magnificent green colors, such as pork cutlets atop a lemony pea mash and whole-wheat spaghetti tossed with arugula-mint pesto.

march

SPICY VEGETABLE HASH

serves 4–6

MARCH

Here, we liven up traditional potato hash with colorful vegetables and spicy flavors. Rather than an all-white potato base, orange-fleshed sweet potatoes are added, which are known to help stabilize blood sugar and aid metabolism. The dish is topped with a medley of fresh nutrient-rich garnishes— yogurt, lime, and fresh cilantro.

1½ lb (750 g) orange-fleshed sweet potatoes, peeled and cut into small cubes

1½ lb (750 g) Yukon gold potatoes, peeled and cut into small cubes

2 Tbsp olive oil

1 medium yellow onion, chopped

1 red bell pepper, seeded and chopped

1 jalapeño chile, seeded and minced

1 cup (6 oz/185 g) fresh or thawed frozen corn kernels

1½ tsp ground cumin

3 Tbsp chopped fresh cilantro, plus more for garnish

Salt and freshly ground pepper

Plain yogurt, for serving

Lime wedges, for serving

Preheat the oven to 400°F (200°C).

Lightly oil a large rimmed baking sheet. Place the sweet and Yukon gold potatoes on the sheet and toss with 1 tablespoon of the oil. Roast for 30 minutes. Using a metal spatula, turn the potatoes, and continue roasting until lightly browned and tender, about 15 minutes longer. Keep warm.

Meanwhile, in a large frying pan, heat the remaining 1 tablespoon oil over medium heat. Add the onion, bell pepper, and jalapeño. Cook, stirring occasionally, until the vegetables are tender, about 10 minutes. Stir in the corn and cook until heated through, about 3 minutes. Stir in the cumin and cook until fragrant, about 30 seconds. Add the reserved potatoes and 3 Tbsp cilantro and stir to combine. Season with salt and pepper.

Divide the hash among individual bowls, topping each serving with a dollop of yogurt and a sprinkle of cilantro. Serve with the lime wedges.

STIR-FRIED PORK & SUGAR SNAPS WITH SOBA NOODLES

serves 2

MARCH

Crunchy sugar snap peas, young green onions, and just a small amount of pork are the basis for this novel dish made with Japanese buckwheat noodles and bold Asian flavors. If you're eating gluten-free, check the label of the soba noodles to make sure they're free of wheat.

4 Tbsp (2 fl oz/60 ml) low-sodium soy sauce

1½ tsp cornstarch

1½ tsp Asian sesame oil, plus 1 Tbsp

½ lb (250 g) boneless center-cut pork chops, cut across the grain into thin strips

Freshly ground pepper

2 Tbsp rice wine vinegar

1½ tsp sugar

½ lb (250 g) sugar snap peas, trimmed and halved on the diagonal

6 oz (185 g) soba noodles

1 bunch green onions, thinly sliced

1 Tbsp peanut oil

1 Tbsp minced peeled fresh ginger

¼ tsp red pepper flakes

In a bowl, combine 2 Tbsp of the soy sauce with the cornstarch and stir to dissolve. Mix in the 1½ tsp sesame oil. Add the pork and a generous amount of pepper and stir to coat. Let marinate for 15–30 minutes. Meanwhile, in a small bowl, combine the remaining 2 Tbsp soy sauce and 1 Tbsp sesame oil with the vinegar and sugar, and stir to dissolve.

Bring a large pot of water to a boil. Add the sugar snap peas and cook until just tender-crisp, about 4 minutes. Using a slotted spoon, transfer the peas to a bowl. Add the noodles to the boiling water and cook until just tender, stirring occasionally, about 4 minutes. Drain the noodles, and return to the pot along with half the sauce. Stir to coat. Mix in the sugar snap peas and all but 2 Tbsp of the green onions. Cover to keep warm.

In a large nonstick frying pan over medium-high heat, warm the peanut oil. Add the ginger and pepper flakes and stir until fragrant, about 5 seconds. Add the pork with the marinade and separate the pieces. Stir constantly until the pork is just cooked through, 2–3 minutes. Add the remaining sauce and stir until the sauce thickens, about 30 seconds. Immediately add the pork and sauce to the noodles, and then toss to coat. Divide the noodles between 2 warmed plates. Sprinkle with the remaining green onions and serve.

3

BLACK BEAN–JALAPEÑO BURGERS WITH AVOCADO MASH

serves 4

1 can (14½ oz/455 g) black beans

2 tsp olive oil

¼ cup (1½ oz/45 g) minced yellow onion

1 small jalapeño chile, ribs and seeds removed, minced

1 Tbsp ground cumin

1 tsp dried oregano

1 tsp salt

1 egg, slightly beaten

6 Tbsp (⅔ oz/20 g) whole-wheat panko bread crumbs

FOR THE AVOCADO MASH

2 ripe avocados

1 Roma tomato, seeded and diced

Juice of 1 lime

Salt

Nonstick cooking spray

This meatless burger is served without a bun to cut down on extra carbs and calories. Avocados lend color and good-for-you fat atop these spicy patties. This is an ideal party dish because the burgers can be made ahead and refrigerated overnight. Try serving them in lettuce cups for a portable meal.

Drain and rinse the black beans, then lay them on paper towels and pat dry. Put the beans in a bowl and mash with a fork, leaving the mixture somewhat chunky.

In a small frying pan over medium heat, warm the oil. Add the onion and jalapeño and cook until soft, about 3 minutes. Add the cumin, oregano, and salt and sauté until aromatic, about 1 minute. Transfer to the bowl with the black beans and stir in the egg and panko. Form into 4 patties and transfer to the refrigerator to chill for 30 minutes.

To make the avocado mash, put the avocado in a bowl. Using a fork, mash well. Stir in the tomato and lime juice and season to taste with salt.

Warm a nonstick frying pan to medium-high heat and lightly coat with nonstick cooking spray. Cook the burgers until heated through and golden-brown, about 5 minutes per side.

Arrange the burgers on plates, top with the avocado mash, and serve.

4

TANDOORI-STYLE CHICKEN

serves 6

1½ tsp *each* cayenne pepper and paprika

Salt and freshly ground pepper

6 skinless, boneless chicken breasts

Juice of 1 lemon

1 small onion, roughly chopped

2 Tbsp peeled and chopped fresh ginger

2 cloves garlic

½ cup (4 oz/125 g) low-fat plain Greek yogurt

1 tsp garam masala

¼ cup (2 fl oz/60 ml) low-fat milk

Olive oil, for brushing

Tandoori chicken is traditionally baked in a "tandoor" oven. Here it's grilled to mimic the high heat of the specialized oven. The chicken is marinated in bold Indian flavors and yogurt, which help to tenderize the meat. Serve this dish with a cooling cucumber-mint sauce (page 134), brown rice, and simmered fresh peas.

In a small bowl, stir together ½ tsp each of the cayenne, paprika, salt, and pepper.

Trim off the tenders from the chicken breasts and reserve for another use. Working with one piece at a time, lay a breast between two pieces of plastic wrap. Use a meat pounder to pound to an even thickness. Place the chicken in a large nonreactive bowl and season with the spice rub, massaging it into the meat. Add the lemon juice and turn to coat. Cover and refrigerate for 30 minutes.

In a food processor, combine the onion, ginger, and garlic. Pulse several times to finely chop. Add the yogurt and the garam masala and continue to pulse until well combined. Add the milk, 1 Tbsp at a time, as needed to thin.

Remove the chicken from the lemon juice and pat dry with paper towels; discard the lemon juice. Return the chicken to the bowl, add the yogurt mixture, and turn to coat. Cover and refrigerate, turning occasionally, for 1–2 hours. Remove from the refrigerator 15 minutes before grilling.

Prepare a grill for direct-heat cooking over medium-high heat. Brush the grill grate with oil. Arrange the chicken breasts on the grill grate, discarding the marinade. Grill, turning once, until grill-marked and charred, 2–3 minutes per side. Move the chicken to the edge of the grill where the heat is less intense. Cover and grill until firm to the touch and cooked through, 3–5 minutes longer. Let rest for 5 minutes.

Slice the chicken, and serve.

5

TOFU & VEGETABLE BUNDLES WITH HOISIN & GINGER

serves 6

1 lb (500 g) extra-firm tofu, diced

1 red pepper, seeds and ribs removed, thinly sliced

1 yellow pepper, seeds and ribs removed, thinly sliced

1 small yellow onion, halved and thinly sliced

3 carrots, cut into 1-inch (2.5-cm) long matchsticks

1 cup (8 oz/250 g) hoisin sauce

2-inch (5-cm) piece fresh ginger, peeled and grated

3 cloves garlic, minced

1 Tbsp rice wine vinegar

½ tsp sesame oil

¼ tsp freshly ground pepper

Tofu is a plant-based protein made from soybeans, and is full of heart-healthy fats and isoflavones, which are known to help prevent cancer and heart disease. Flavors are absorbed easily through tofu's porous surface, making it an ideal vehicle for this Asian-style marinade. Serve the bundles over steamed brown rice or soba noodles for a more filling meal.

Preheat the oven to 375°F (190°C). In a large bowl, place the tofu, red pepper, yellow pepper, onion, and carrots. Add the hoisin, ginger, garlic, vinegar, sesame oil, and pepper and gently toss to coat.

Cut out six 12-inch (30-cm) square pieces of parchment. Working with one piece at a time, pile one-sixth of the mixture in the center. Working with two parallel sides at a time, bring two edges together at the center atop the mixture, and fold them over to seal. Repeat with the remaining two short edges, folding them over at the center, forming a smaller square. Repeat with the remaining 5 pieces of parchment. Carefully transfer the bundles to a baking sheet, placing them seam-side down. Bake until the vegetables soften and begin to caramelize, 25–30 minutes.

Place the packets on warmed plates. Carefully slit an X in the top of each packet to let the steam escape, and serve.

6

SOUTHERN-STYLE CATFISH WITH BRAISED COLLARD GREENS

serves 4

4 catfish fillets, about 1½ lb (750 g) total

Salt and freshly ground black pepper

½ cup (4 fl oz/125 ml) buttermilk

1 cup (5 oz/155 g) fine yellow cornmeal

¼ tsp cayenne pepper

3 Tbsp peanut or canola oil

1 yellow onion, halved and thinly sliced

2 bunches collard greens, about 1 lb (500 g) total, ribs removed and shredded

1 clove garlic, sliced

2 lemons, cut into wedges

This southern-inspired dish is full of homey flavors, like buttermilk, cornmeal, and garlic. Tender greens and lightly battered fish make a great combination. Serve this dish with corn bread and hot sauce for an authentic down-south meal. You can also use mustard or turnip greens in place of collards—they both have a similar nutritional punch.

Put the fillets in a baking dish and season lightly with salt and black pepper. Add the buttermilk and let stand for 5–10 minutes. In another baking dish, stir together the cornmeal and cayenne.

In a deep frying pan over low heat, warm 1 Tbsp of the oil. Add the onion and sauté until softened, about 10 minutes. Raise the heat to medium, add the greens and garlic, cover, and cook, stirring occasionally, until the greens are tender, about 15 minutes. Season with salt and pepper and keep warm.

Meanwhile, in a large frying pan over medium heat, warm the remaining 2 Tbsp oil. Lift each fillet from the buttermilk, letting any excess drip into the bowl. Dredge the fillets in the cornmeal mixture, shaking off any excess. Cook until golden-brown, about 4 minutes. Turn and cook until cooked through, 2–3 minutes. Drain on paper towels.

Arrange the fillets on plates, and serve with the greens and lemon wedges.

7

CHICKEN BREASTS WITH FAVA BEANS

serves 4

2 lb (1 kg) fava beans in their pods, shelled

4 boneless, skinless chicken breast halves, about 6 oz (185 g) each

Salt and freshly ground pepper

2 Tbsp *each* extra-virgin olive oil and unsalted butter

4 green onions, chopped, white and green parts separated

1 clove garlic, minced

¼ cup (2 fl oz/60 ml) dry white wine

¾ cup (6 fl oz/180 m) low-sodium chicken broth

This light meal features low-fat skinless chicken and a whole lot of green. If you're not up for the labor of preparing fava beans, peas can be substituted in a pinch. Just add fresh or thawed frozen peas after deglazing the pan with wine.

Bring a saucepan three-fourths full of water to a boil and add the favas. Boil for 1 minute, then drain. Squeeze each bean free of its tough outer skin.

Preheat the oven to 200°F (95°C). Using a meat pounder, pound each chicken breast to an even thickness. Season the breasts with 1 tsp salt and ½ tsp pepper.

In a large frying pan, warm the oil over medium-high heat. Add the chicken and cook until golden brown, 3–4 minutes. Turn and cook until the other side is golden and the chicken springs back when pressed, about 4 minutes. Transfer to a rimmed baking sheet and keep warm in the oven.

Pour off the fat from the pan and return it to medium-high heat. Add 1 Tbsp of the butter, and allow it to melt. Add the white parts of the green onions and the garlic and sauté until softened, about 2 minutes. Add the wine and cook, scraping up the browned bits from the pan bottom, until almost evaporated, about 30 seconds. Add the fava beans and ¼ cup (2 fl oz/ 60 ml) of the broth, cover, and cook, stirring occasionally, until tender, about 3 minutes. Stir in the remaining ½ cup (4 fl oz/125 ml) broth and bring to a boil. Remove from the heat and stir in the remaining 1 Tbsp butter. Taste and adjust the seasonings.

Cut each chicken breast across the grain into slices and transfer to warmed plates. Spoon some of the fava beans and sauce over each breast. Sprinkle with the green onion tops, and serve.

8

CONCHIGLIE WITH KALE & WHITE BEANS

serves 4–6

1½ lb (750 g) Tuscan kale

Salt

6 Tbsp (3 fl oz/90 ml) extra-virgin olive oil

6 large cloves garlic, smashed

2 oz (60 g) sliced pancetta or bacon, finely diced (optional)

¼ tsp red pepper flakes

1 can (14 oz/440 g) cannellini beans, drained and well rinsed

½ lb (250 g) conchiglie (medium pasta shells)

It's essential to remove the tough, inedible stems of kale and leave behind only the fiber-dense leaves. This one-pot meal uses a good portion of olive oil. So long as you use one of good quality, don't fret about the quantity, as olive oil has been shown to help maintain good cholesterol levels in your system.

Using a long, sharp knife, cut off the tough stems from the kale, then fold each leaf in half lengthwise and slice off the tough central rib. Cut crosswise into ribbons about 2 inches (5 cm) wide.

Bring a large pot of salted water to a boil.

In a frying pan large enough to hold the pasta later, warm the oil over medium heat. Add the garlic and pancetta, if using, and sauté until both are lightly colored, about 5 minutes. Add the kale, toss to coat with the oil, and sauté until wilted, about 7 minutes. Add ¾ cup (6 fl oz/180 ml) water, a scant ½ tsp salt, and the red pepper flakes; mix well, cover, and cook until the kale is nearly tender, about 5 minutes. Add the beans, re-cover, reduce the heat to low, and cook until the beans are heated through, about 5 minutes. Remove from the heat and cover to keep warm.

While the sauce is cooking, add the pasta to the boiling water, stir, and cook, stirring occasionally, until al dente, about 10 minutes, or according to package directions.

Drain the pasta, add it to the sauce in the pan, and toss well to combine. Taste and adjust the seasoning with salt. Transfer to a warmed large, shallow serving bowl or individual shallow bowls, and serve.

MOREL & LEEK RAVIOLI WITH ENGLISH PEA PURÉE

serves 6

Fresh pasta sheets are stuffed with seasonal vegetables and rest atop a bed of bright mashed peas for an exceptionally springy meal. These ravioli are heavy on the vegetables and light on the cheese, making them healthier than meat-and dairy-laden versions.

2 Tbsp extra-virgin olive oil

2 Tbsp unsalted butter

½ cup (1½ oz/45 g) thinly sliced leeks

Salt and freshly ground pepper

1 lb (500 g) fresh morel mushrooms

1 tsp minced fresh thyme

1 cup (8 oz/250 g) fresh ricotta cheese

½ cup (2 oz/60 g) freshly grated pecorino romano cheese

12 oz (375 g) fresh pasta sheets, 10-by-5 inches (23-by-13 cm)

All-purpose flour, for dusting

2 lb (1 kg) fresh English peas, shelled

1 cup (8 fl oz/250 ml) low-sodium chicken broth

2 tsp fresh lemon juice

¼ cup (2 oz/60 g) minced fresh chives

Warm a sauté pan over medium heat. Add 1 Tbsp of the oil and 1 Tbsp of the butter. When the butter melts, add the leeks and a pinch each of salt and pepper. Sauté until translucent, 4–5 minutes. Coarsely chop half of the morels and add them to the pan with another pinch of salt. Sauté until the mushrooms have softened, 3–4 minutes. Add the thyme and sauté for 1 minute. Transfer the mixture to a bowl. When slightly cool, stir in the ricotta and half of the pecorino. Season with salt and pepper.

Lay a pasta sheet horizontally on a work surface. Place tablespoons of the filling along the bottom half of the dough, spaced 1½ inches (4 cm) apart and leaving a border of about ½ inch (12 mm) around the edge. Lightly moisten the edges of the dough with water. Fold the top half of the dough over the filled half, pressing down between the mounds of filling to seal the dough and remove any air pockets. Using a fluted cutter or sharp knife, cut the filled pasta into squares and place them on a lightly floured baking sheet. Repeat with the remaining pasta sheets and filling.

Bring a large pot of generously salted water to a boil over high heat and prepare a bowl of ice water. When the water comes to ⟫⟩

a boil, add the peas and cook until tender, 5–6 minutes. Remove the peas with a strainer or slotted spoon and immediately plunge them into the ice water. When cool, drain and transfer 1 cup of the peas to a food processor. Return the water to a boil.

Add the broth, lemon juice, half of the chives and a pinch of salt and pepper to the food processor and purée the mixture until smooth.

Place the sauté pan back over medium heat and add the remaining oil and butter. Sauté the remaining whole morels with salt and pepper, stirring, until lightly browned and tender, 4–5 minutes. Add the pea purée and remaining peas and reduce the heat to low.

When water comes back to a boil, add half of the ravioli and reduce the heat to medium. Cook just until the ravioli float to the top of the water, 2–3 minutes. Remove the ravioli with a slotted spoon and add them to the pan with the pea purée. If needed, add some of the pasta cooking water to the pea purée to loosen the sauce. The sauce should cling nicely to the ravioli without being too thick. Repeat with the remaining ravioli.

Transfer the ravioli and sauce to a warm serving dish and top with the remaining pecorino and chives.

10

SPRING PEAS WITH BARLEY, CHILE & GREEN ONIONS

serves 4

This super-light version of fried rice swaps rice for heart-healthy barley. This dish is as simple as 1-2-3: Just boil some peas and barley, mix up a flavor-filled Asian sauce, and stir-fry all the ingredients together. Add tofu, shrimp, or leftover grilled chicken for a complete meal.

Salt

6 oz (185 g) sugar snap peas, trimmed

1 cup (5 oz/155 g) shelled English peas

½ cup (3½ oz/105 g) pearl barley

2 Tbsp rice vinegar

2 Tbsp soy sauce

1 Tbsp firmly packed golden brown sugar

1 tsp sambal oelek

1 Tbsp Asian sesame oil

4 cloves garlic, minced

¼ cup (¾ oz/20 g) sliced green onions

2 fresh kaffir lime leaves

¼ lb (125 g) pea shoots

Bring a large saucepan half full of salted water to a boil over high heat. Add the snap peas and English peas and cook until tender-crisp, about 1 minute. Using a slotted spoon, transfer the vegetables to a colander and rinse under cold water. Set aside. Return the saucepan to a boil, add the barley, and cook until tender, about 45 minutes. Drain and set aside.

In a small bowl, whisk together the vinegar, soy sauce, brown sugar, sambal oelek, and 2 Tbsp water until blended. In a large, heavy frying pan over high heat, warm the sesame oil. Add the garlic, green onions, and lime leaves and stir-fry until the green onions are tender, about 30 seconds. Add the reserved peas and barley along with the pea shoots, and stir to coat. Pour in the soy sauce mixture and toss until the peas and pea shoots are tender and the liquid is absorbed, about 4 minutes.

Transfer to a warmed serving dish, remove the lime leaves, and serve.

11

THAI-STYLE GREEN FISH CURRY

serves 6

Here, white fish simmers in a lemongrass-infused coconut sauce. This dish uses zero oil, because the fish cooks in hot liquid. Poaching in coconut milk is a great way to add flavor and heart-healthy fats to your meals.

1½ lb (750 g) firm white fish fillets such as halibut, cod, or sea bass, each about 1½ inches (4 cm) thick, skinned

1 stalk fresh lemongrass

1 can (14 fl oz/430 ml) unsweetened coconut milk

1 cup (8 fl oz/250 ml) reduced-sodium chicken broth

3 tbsp Asian fish sauce

Finely grated zest of 1 lime

3 Tbsp fresh lime juice

1 Tbsp Thai green curry paste

1 Tbsp peeled and grated fresh ginger

1 clove garlic, minced

½ cup (⅔ oz/20 g) chopped fresh cilantro

¼ cup (⅓ oz/10 g) chopped fresh basil

2 Tbsp chopped fresh mint

Cooked brown basmati rice for serving

Cut the fillets into 1½-inch (4-cm) chunks and set aside.

Cut off about 2 inches (5 cm) of the lemongrass stem and pull off and discard the tough outside layers. Finely mince the tender inside stalks, measure out 1 tsp, and add it to a saucepan. Add the coconut milk, broth, fish sauce, lime zest and juice, curry paste, ginger, and garlic.

Bring the coconut milk mixture to a boil over medium-high heat, then reduce the heat to low and simmer, uncovered, for about 10 minutes to blend the flavors. Add the fish and simmer gently until the fish is opaque throughout when tested with a knife tip, 4–5 minutes. Add the cilantro, basil, and mint. Taste the curry and adjust the seasonings with fish sauce.

Serve over rice in warmed shallow bowls.

12

Because this pizza relies on healthy pantry staples, it's a great, quick option for easy weeknight dinners when your refrigerator is bare. Serve this pizza with a green salad for a balanced meal.

FOUR-SEASONS PIZZA

serves 2–4

All-purpose flour and cornmeal, for dusting

1 lb (500 g) purchased whole-wheat pizza dough

½ cup (4 fl oz/125 ml) tomato sauce

1 jarred roasted red bell pepper, cut into strips

2 white mushrooms, brushed clean and thinly sliced

2 jarred artichoke hearts, drained and thinly sliced

6 black olives, pitted and thinly sliced

2 Tbsp olive oil

2 fresh basil leaves, torn into small pieces

Position a rack in the bottom of the oven. Place a baking stone on the rack. Preheat the oven to 550°F (290°C), or the highest setting, for at least 45 minutes.

To assemble the pizza, lightly flour a work surface. Roll the dough into a round 13–14 inches (33–35 cm) in diameter. Generously dust a pizza peel or rimless baking sheet with cornmeal and transfer the dough round to it. Working quickly, spread the tomato sauce on the dough, leaving a ½-inch (12-mm) border uncovered. Visualize the pizza in 4 equal wedges and arrange the pepper strips, mushrooms, artichoke slices, and olives each in their own quadrant. Drizzle with the oil.

Immediately slide the pizza from the peel onto the baking stone. Bake until the crust is crisp and browned, about 8 minutes. Remove from the oven. Sprinkle with the basil, and serve.

13

Salmon is a terrific source of omega-3 fatty acids, which are associated with heart health. Nutrient-dense quinoa has a mild flavor and light, fluffy texture which pairs well with rich salmon and slightly bitter parsley. Both salmon and quinoa are packed with protein and are quick and easy to prepare. Ask your fishmonger for center-cut salmon to ensure the pieces are the same thickness throughout, which will help them to cook evenly.

SALMON WITH QUINOA & PARSLEY VINAIGRETTE

serves 4

Salt and freshly ground pepper

1 cup (8 oz/250 g) quinoa, rinsed

4 salmon fillets (4–6 oz/125–185 g each)

2 Tbsp olive oil, plus 2 tsp for brushing

3 Tbsp red wine vinegar

2 tsp Dijon mustard

½ cup (¾ oz/20 g) chopped fresh flat-leaf parsley

In a saucepan, bring 2 cups (16 fl oz/ 500 ml) water to a boil over high heat. Add a big pinch of salt and the quinoa. Return to a boil and then reduce the heat to low. Cover and cook until all the liquid is absorbed, about 12 minutes. Using a fork, fluff the quinoa. Put the lid back on and let stand for 15 minutes.

Warm a stove-top grill pan over medium-high heat. Brush the salmon with 2 tsp oil and season well with salt and pepper. Place the salmon on the pan, flesh side down, and cook for 5 minutes. Flip the salmon over, and cook until done to your liking, about 4 minutes more for medium. Transfer to a plate.

In a small bowl combine the vinegar, mustard, ½ tsp salt, and ⅛ tsp pepper. Slowly whisk in the remaining 2 Tbsp oil and stir in the parsley to make a vinaigrette. Stir 3 Tbsp of the vinaigrette into the quinoa.

Divide the quinoa among 4 warmed plates. Top each plate with a piece of grilled salmon, drizzle the remaining vinaigrette over the top, and serve.

14

Egg salad gets a healthy makeover in this mayo-free version. Chard adds color and nutrients, while cayenne and garlic bring new flavor to the classic dish. A small amount of bacon, about ½ slice per person, lends savoriness without a lot of extra fat.

CHOPPED CHARD & EGG SALAD
serves 4

2 bunches Swiss chard

Salt and freshly ground black pepper

2 slices thick-sliced bacon, coarsely chopped

3 Tbsp extra-virgin olive oil

1 clove garlic, minced

Pinch of cayenne pepper

4 Tbsp (2 fl oz/60 ml) balsamic vinegar

2 Tbsp red wine vinegar

4 Tbsp (⅓ oz/10 g) chopped fresh flat-leaf parsley

4 hard-boiled eggs, peeled and coarsely chopped

Cut out the ribs from the chard leaves. Trim the rib ends, then chop the ribs into small pieces. Bring a large saucepan three-fourths full of water to a boil over medium-high heat. Add 1 tsp salt and the chopped chard ribs and cook until just tender, 7 minutes. Using a slotted spoon, lift out the ribs, draining them well, and set aside. Add the leaves to the same boiling water and cook just until tender to the bite, 5 minutes. Drain and rinse under cold running water until cool. Gently squeeze the leaves dry with your hands, then coarsely chop them. Gently squeeze them in your hands again. Set aside.

Place a frying pan over medium heat. When it is hot, add the bacon and cook, turning occasionally, until nearly golden, 5 minutes. Pour off the rendered fat. Add 1 Tbsp of the oil, the garlic, and cayenne and continue to cook until the bacon and garlic are golden. Using a slotted spoon, transfer the bacon and garlic to a paper towel to drain.

Add 2 Tbsp of the balsamic vinegar to the frying pan and deglaze it, stirring to scrape up bits from the pan bottom. Pour into a large serving bowl. Add the remaining 2 Tbsp oil and balsamic vinegar and the red wine vinegar and mix well. Add the reserved chard leaves and ribs, the bacon and garlic, 3 Tbsp of the parsley, and ½ tsp black pepper. Mix well. Stir in the eggs. Garnish with the remaining 1 Tbsp parsley, and serve.

15

This is an easy after-school or work meal or a novel dish to serve at dinner parties. Dark-meat turkey has more fat than light-meat, keeping you fuller for longer. Here it's stir-fried with simple Asian seasonings, and scooped into cup-like butter lettuce leaves for crunch and extra nutrients.

TURKEY LETTUCE WRAPS
serves 4

1 Tbsp *each* canola oil and Asian sesame oil

½ cup (1½ oz/45 g) thinly sliced green onion

1½ Tbsp grated fresh ginger

2 cloves garlic, minced

½ tsp red pepper flakes

1¼ lb (750 g) ground dark-meat turkey

3 Tbsp low-sodium soy sauce

1 Tbsp rice vinegar

16 butter lettuce leaves (from 2 small heads)

Torn fresh basil leaves, for garnish

Hoisin sauce, for serving (optional)

Warm the oils in a large frying pan over medium-high heat. Add the green onion, ginger, garlic, and red pepper flakes and cook, stirring constantly, until fragrant, about 2 minutes. Add the turkey and cook, stirring to break into pieces, until the turkey is cooked through, about 5 minutes. Add the soy sauce and vinegar and cook 1 minute more. Transfer the mixture to a bowl.

To serve, spoon a small amount of the turkey mixture into the center of each lettuce leaf, dividing evenly. Top with basil, and wrap each lettuce leaf around the filling. Drizzle with hoisin sauce to taste, if desired.

16

Pea shoots, the clippings from young pea plants, have a mild pealike flavor that blends well with peppery watercress. Pea shoots are sold in Asian markets, but if you can't find them, you can substitute baby arugula or spinach.

PAN-SEARED SALMON WITH SPRING GREENS

serves 8

⅔ cup (5 fl oz/160 ml) extra-virgin olive oil

⅓ cup (3 fl oz/80 ml) Meyer lemon juice or regular lemon juice

3 shallots, minced

Salt and freshly ground pepper

¼ tsp sugar, if needed

5 cups (5 oz/155 g) watercress leaves

5 cups (5 oz/155 g) pea shoots

FOR THE SALMON

Salt and freshly ground pepper

8 skinless salmon fillets, each about ⅓ lb (5 oz/155 g) and ½ inch (12 mm) thick

½ cup (4 fl oz/125 ml) dry white wine

8 Tbsp (4 fl oz/125 ml) Meyer lemon juice or regular lemon juice

In a large bowl, combine the olive oil, lemon juice, shallots, ½ tsp salt, and ½ tsp pepper. Add the sugar if using regular lemon juice. Mix until well blended. Add the watercress leaves and pea shoots and turn gently to coat well. Divide the greens evenly among 8 plates.

To prepare the salmon, sprinkle 1½ tsp salt in a wide, heavy frying pan and place over medium-high heat until nearly smoking. Add the salmon fillets and sear for 2 minutes on one side. Turn and sear for 1 minute on the second side. Sprinkle with 1 tsp pepper. Reduce the heat to low, then pour in the wine and 2 Tbsp of the lemon juice. Cover and cook until the juices are nearly absorbed and the fish is halfway cooked, about 3 minutes. Uncover and pour in 2 more Tbsp of the lemon juice and 3 Tbsp water. Re-cover and cook just until the fish flakes easily with a fork, about 3 minutes longer. Most of the pan juices will have been absorbed.

Place a salmon fillet on each mound of greens. Raise the heat to high, add the remaining 4 Tbsp lemon juice and 1 Tbsp water and stir to scrape up the browned bits from the pan bottom. Pour the pan juices evenly over the fish, and serve.

17

To cut meat thinly, freeze it for about 20 minutes, or just until it's firm. The thinner the cut, the quicker the steak cooks, helping this simple, yet elegant, meal come together in minutes. Serve this dish with a side of roasted sweet potatoes for a balanced meal.

BEEF WITH ARUGULA & HERBS

serves 2

1 bunch arugula, stems removed

1 Tbsp chopped fresh chives

1 tsp chopped fresh rosemary

1 tsp chopped fresh thyme

1 Tbsp olive oil

½ lb (250 g) boneless lean steak, partially frozen and thinly sliced against the grain

Salt and freshly ground pepper

Aged balsamic vinegar for drizzling

Divide the arugula between 2 plates. In a small bowl, mix together the chives, rosemary, and thyme.

Warm a large, heavy frying pan over medium heat until very hot. Add the oil. When the oil is hot, place the beef slices in the pan in a single layer. Cook, without disturbing, until the beef is browned on the first side, about 2 minutes. Turn the meat over and season with salt and pepper. Cook until browned on the second side, about 1 minute longer.

Arrange the beef slices on top of the arugula, sprinkle with the herbs, drizzle with balsamic vinegar, and serve.

GARLICKY SHRIMP & CHARD SAUTÉ

serves 4

1 lb (500 g) large shrimp,
peeled and deveined

Salt

3 Tbsp extra-virgin olive oil

2 bunches chard, thick ribs removed,
chopped

2 Tbsp chopped garlic

½ tsp red pepper flakes

Grated zest and juice of 1 orange

1 bay leaf

2 Tbsp minced fresh flat-leaf parsley

*Chard and
shrimp are both
complimented by
acidic ingredients.
In this recipe,
we swapped the
usual lemon juice
for the zest and juice
of an orange.
The orange juice
is used to deglaze
the pan after
sautéing the shrimp,
which results in
a sweet and savory
sauce that is
poured over
the finished dish.*

Place the shrimp in a bowl, add 1 tsp salt, and toss to coat. Refrigerate for 15 minutes.

In a frying pan over high heat, heat half of the oil. Add the chard, 1 Tbsp of the garlic, ¼ tsp of the red pepper flakes, and ¼ tsp salt. Sauté until the chard is wilted and tender, about 3 minutes. Transfer to a warmed platter and sprinkle with the orange zest. Cover to keep warm.

Add the remaining oil to the pan. When the oil shimmers, add the shrimp, the remaining 1 Tbsp garlic, the remaining ¼ tsp red pepper flakes, and the bay leaf and sauté until the shrimp starts to turn opaque, about 1 minute. Add the orange juice and continue to sauté, stirring to dislodge the browned bits on the bottom of the pan, until the shrimp is opaque throughout, about 1 minute more.

Arrange the shrimp on top of the chard and drizzle the orange sauce over the top. Garnish with the parsley, and serve.

PAN-GRILLED ASPARAGUS & ENDIVE WITH FAVA BEANS, ORANGE & BASIL

serves 4

3 lb (1.5 kg) fava beans, outer pods removed

1 lb (500 g) slender asparagus, trimmed

2 heads Belgian endive, sliced
lengthwise ⅛ inch (3 mm) thick

2 Tbsp olive oil

Salt and freshly ground pepper

2 oranges

2 Tbsp extra-virgin olive oil

½ cup (½ oz/15 g) small fresh basil leaves

*This dish makes
a beautiful party
platter or addition
to any spring meal.
Grilling the endive
and asparagus and
preparing the favas
and oranges simply
allows each element
of the dish to pop.
A super-light orange
juice-based dressing
allows the bright
colors and fresh
tastes to stand
out in this salad.*

Bring a saucepan three-fourths full of water to a boil and add the favas. Boil for 1 minute, then drain. Squeeze each bean free of its tough outer skin.

Warm a stove-top grill pan over medium-high heat. Put the asparagus and endive slices in a bowl, add the olive oil, and toss to coat thoroughly. Add the asparagus and endive to the hot grill pan and cook, turning occasionally, until the vegetables are charred and tender-crisp, 8–10 minutes total. Season the vegetables well with salt and pepper.

Finely grate the zest from 1 orange over a bowl. Cut a slice off both ends of 1 orange so it will stand upright. Stand it on a cutting board and, using a large, sharp knife, cut away the peel and white pith by slicing from top to bottom, following the contour of the fruit. Cut the orange crosswise into thin rounds.

Cut the second orange in half and squeeze the juice into another bowl. Whisk in the extra-virgin olive oil and season with salt and pepper to make a dressing.

Arrange the asparagus, endive, oranges, and fava beans on a platter. Sprinkle with the reserved orange zest and basil. Drizzle with some of the orange dressing, and serve.

SAUTÉED PORK CUTLETS WITH LEMONY PEA MASH

serves 4

2 Tbsp plus 1 tsp olive oil

2 cloves garlic, minced

3 cups (15 oz/470 g) fresh shelled English peas or thawed frozen peas

Grated zest and juice of 1 lemon

Salt and freshly ground pepper

1 lb (500 g) pork cutlets, pounded until ⅛ inch (3 mm) thick

This is a quick go-to meal you can feel good about. Fibrous peas are a colorful replacement for potatoes in this lemony mash. Rich in antioxidants and anti-inflammatory compounds, and low in calories, peas make a guilt-free base to any meal. Pounding pork cutlets helps the meat cook quickly and evenly.

In a frying pan, warm 2 Tbsp oil over medium-high heat. Add the garlic and sauté just until aromatic, about 1 minute. Add the peas and stir to combine. Sauté until the peas begin to soften, about 2 minutes. Stir in the lemon zest and juice and cook until the peas absorb the liquid, 1–2 more minutes. Season well with salt and pepper. Transfer the pea mixture to a food processor and purée until smooth. Set aside.

Wipe the frying pan clean with a paper towel and warm it over high heat. Season both sides of the pork cutlets with salt and pepper. When the frying pan is very hot, add the remaining 1 tsp oil and the pork cutlets and sauté until they are opaque throughout, about 2 minutes per side.

To serve, divide the pea mash among 4 plates and top with the pork cutlets.

TOFU-VEGETABLE FRIED RICE

serves 4–6

4 Tbsp (2 fl oz/60 ml) peanut or canola oil

2 eggs, lightly beaten

½ lb (250 g) firm tofu, cut into ½-inch (12-mm) cubes

1 Tbsp balsamic vinegar

1 leek, including light green tops, finely chopped

1 cup (2 oz/60 g) broccoli florets

1 carrot, cut into 1-inch (2.5-cm) pieces

2 cups (6 oz/185 g) finely chopped napa cabbage

1 Tbsp dry sherry

4 cups (1¼ lb/625 g) cooked brown rice, cold

¼ cup (2 fl oz/60 ml) low-sodium vegetable broth

2 Tbsp low-sodium soy sauce

2 Tbsp thinly sliced green onions

This dish is a great way to use up bits of vegetables in your refrigerator. Don't feel constrained to the ingredients listed here—any favorite vegetables can be used and a colorful assortment will guarantee a range of nutrients.

Warm a wok or large frying pan over medium heat. Swirl in 1 Tbsp of the oil. When the oil is hot, add the eggs and stir until soft curds form, about 1 minute. Transfer to a bowl.

Return the pan to medium-high heat. Swirl in another 1 Tbsp oil. When hot, add the tofu and stir-fry until it begins to brown, 4–5 minutes. Add the vinegar and cook, stirring once, for 30 seconds. Add to the bowl with the eggs.

Return the pan to medium-high heat. Swirl in another 1 Tbsp oil. When hot, add the leeks and stir-fry until slightly softened, 2–3 minutes. Add the broccoli, carrots, and cabbage and stir-fry until the vegetables just begin to soften, 2–3 minutes. Add the sherry and cook for 1 minute longer. Add the mixture to the bowl with the eggs and tofu.

Swirl the remaining 1 Tbsp oil into the pan over medium-high heat. Break up any clumps in the rice and add to the hot pan. Stir-fry until lightly browned, about 5 minutes. Add the broth, soy sauce, and green onions and stir. Add the reserved tofu, vegetables, and eggs and stir-fry until the eggs are in small pieces and the mixture is heated through, about 1 minute longer. Taste and adjust the seasonings. Transfer to a warmed platter, and serve.

22

Arugula gets its peppery bite from sulfur-based cancer-fighting phyto-chemicals. With just 5 calories per cup, this zesty green makes a healthy and unique base for pesto. Make extra for spreading on whole-grain crostini and roasted vegetables.

SPAGHETTI WITH ARUGULA-MINT PESTO

serves 4

5 cups (5 oz/155 g) packed arugula

¾ cup (½ oz/15 g) packed fresh mint leaves

½ cup (4 fl oz/125 ml) extra-virgin olive oil

½ cup (2 oz/60 g) Parmesan cheese, plus more for serving

2 cloves garlic

Grated zest and juice of 1 lemon

Salt and freshly ground pepper

1 lb (500 g) multigrain spaghetti

In a blender, combine the arugula, mint, oil, cheese, garlic, lemon zest, and salt and pepper to taste and blend until smooth. Stir in 1 Tbsp of the lemon juice and adjust the seasoning. Refrigerate until ready to serve.

Bring a large pot of salted water to a boil. Add the spaghetti and cook until al dente, 10–12 minutes or according to the package directions. Reserve ½ cup (4 fl oz/125 ml) of the pasta cooking water. Drain the pasta and return it to the empty pot.

Toss the spaghetti with the pesto. Thin it with a small amount of pasta water, if necessary. Taste, season with salt and pepper, and toss with 1 Tbsp lemon juice. Divide among serving bowls.

Sprinkle cheese over each bowl, and serve.

23

This classic chicken curry is swimming in flavor. The chicken is simmered in coconut milk, which also serves as the base of this heavily-scented curry sauce. Add a few packed cups of fresh spinach to the sauce to increase your vegetable intake for the day.

CHICKEN-COCONUT CURRY

serves 4–6

2 lemongrass stalks

2 Tbsp canola oil

1 small yellow onion, halved and thinly sliced

1 heaping Tbsp grated fresh ginger

2 cloves garlic, pressed

¼ tsp ground cumin

1 Tbsp firmly packed light brown sugar

1 can (14.5 fl oz/430 ml) coconut milk

½ cup (4 fl oz/125 ml) low-sodium chicken broth

2–3 Tbsp Asian fish sauce

2 kaffir lime leaves

1 lb (500 g) boneless, skinless chicken breasts or thighs, thinly sliced

½ cup (¾ oz/20 g) firmly packed fresh basil leaves

1 cup (3 oz/90 g) thinly sliced white mushrooms

2 Tbsp lime juice

Hot cooked brown jasmine or basmati rice for serving

Cilantro sprigs and lime wedges for serving

Trim the lemongrass to the white bulb only, then slice in half lengthwise and crush it with the side of your knife. Heat a saucepan over medium-high heat and add the oil. When the oil is hot, add the onion, lemongrass, ginger, and garlic, and sauté until the garlic is golden, 1–2 minutes. Add the cumin and brown sugar, and cook until the sugar bubbles, about 30 seconds. Add the coconut milk, broth, fish sauce, and lime leaves and bring to a boil. Reduce the heat to low, and simmer for 15 minutes to blend the flavors.

Add the chicken, basil, mushrooms, and lime juice and simmer until the chicken is opaque, about 10 minutes longer. Remove and discard the lemongrass stalks.

Spoon the curry over rice in warmed bowls, garnish with cilantro sprigs and lime wedges, and serve.

24

This one-pot meal involves hardly any hands-on time. Just simmer vegetables and beans into a homestyle gumbo, brimming with familiar flavors, and dinner is ready. Serve this dish with cooked brown rice and hot pepper sauce to season to taste.

KALE & RED BEAN GUMBO

serves 4

6 cups (12 oz/ 375 g) chopped kale

1 green bell pepper, seeded and chopped

1 large green onion, chopped

1 cup (7 oz/220 g) canned tomatoes with juice

4 cups (32 fl oz/1 l) vegetable broth

2 dried bay leaves

1 tsp *each* dried oregano and thyme

1 can (15 oz/ 470 g) red beans, drained

8 okra pods, cut into ½-inch (12-mm) pieces

Salt and freshly ground pepper

Combine the kale, bell pepper, green onion, tomatoes, and broth in a heavy-bottomed saucepan or Dutch oven. Add the bay leaves, oregano, and thyme. Bring to a boil over medium-high heat. Reduce the heat to medium-low, cover, and simmer until the kale is tender, about 30 minutes. Add the beans and okra, cover, and cook until the okra is just tender, about 15 minutes. Season with salt and pepper, and serve.

25

Pan-grilling, rather than the classic deep-frying method, makes these falafel healthier. But the real nutrition superstar of this meal is the tahini. This thick paste, made from ground sesame seeds, is a natural source of calcium, known to strengthen bones. For a gluten-free alternative, serve the patties on top of a salad of romaine lettuce, tomatoes, olives, and cucumbers and drizzle the lemon-tahini sauce on top.

FALAFEL BURGERS WITH LEMON-TAHINI SAUCE

serves 8

FOR THE LEMON-TAHINI SAUCE

⅓ cup (3 oz/90 g) tahini

¼ cup (2 fl oz/60 ml) lemon juice

3 Tbsp plain yogurt

1 clove garlic

Salt and freshly ground pepper

FOR THE FALAFEL BURGERS

2 cans (14 oz/440 g each) chickpeas, drained and rinsed

½ red onion, chopped

2 Tbsp fresh flat-leaf parsley leaves

5 fresh mint leaves

2 cloves garlic

Grated zest and juice of 1 lemon

1 Tbsp ground cumin

2 tsp ground coriander

1 tsp paprika

1 tsp salt

½ tsp pepper

1 egg, lightly beaten

½ cup (¾ oz/20 g) whole-wheat panko bread crumbs

Nonstick cooking spray

4 whole-wheat pita breads, toasted, cut in half, and split to form pockets

Thinly sliced red onion, sliced Roma tomatoes, and romaine lettuce, for serving

To make the sauce, in a blender, combine the tahini, lemon juice, yogurt, and garlic and purée until smooth. Season with salt and pepper.

To make the burgers, in a food processor, combine the chickpeas, onion, parsley, mint, garlic, lemon zest and juice, cumin, coriander, paprika, salt, and pepper. Process until smooth and transfer to a large bowl. Add the egg and bread crumbs and stir to combine. Form into 8 patties.

Warm a stove-top grill pan over medium-high heat and coat with cooking spray. Cook the burgers, carefully turning once, until golden-brown, about 4 minutes per side.

To serve, put each burger in a pita pocket, top with a generous helping of sauce, and fill with red onion, tomato slices, and lettuce.

STIR-FRIED HALIBUT WITH FRESH SNOW PEAS

serves 2 or 3

In this fresh take on Asian stir-fry, colorful and nutrient-dense vegetables mingle with quick-cooking halibut in a dish that takes about 30 minutes to prepare from start to finish. The surprise ingredient is lemon marmalade, which adds sweetness and tartness to the dish and gives the sauce extra texture.

⅓ cup (3 fl oz/80 ml) fresh lime juice

1 clove garlic, minced

1 Tbsp finely chopped fresh cilantro

Chile oil

2 tsp prepared lemon marmalade

Salt

1 egg white

1 Tbsp rice wine

2 tsp soy sauce

1 Tbsp cornstarch

1 lb (500 g) halibut fillets, cut into ¾-inch (2-cm) pieces

4 Tbsp (2 fl oz/60 ml) peanut or canola oil

2 green onions, finely chopped

1 tsp minced fresh ginger

¼ lb (125 g) snow peas

2 small carrots, cut into thin strips

In a small bowl, combine the lime juice, garlic, cilantro, a splash of chile oil, the marmalade, and ¼ tsp salt and stir well to make a sauce. Set aside.

In another bowl, stir together the egg white, rice wine, soy sauce, and cornstarch until blended to make a marinade. Add the halibut pieces and toss gently to coat. Set aside.

Warm a wok or large frying pan over high heat. Swirl in 2 Tbsp of the oil. When the oil is hot, add the green onions, ginger, snow peas, and carrots and stir-fry until the vegetables are tender-crisp, 2–3 minutes. Transfer to a plate.

Add the remaining 2 Tbsp oil to the pan. Add the fish with the marinade and stir-fry gently until firm and opaque throughout, 2–3 minutes. Return the vegetables to the pan and stir-fry gently once or twice, cooking for about 30 seconds.

Quickly stir the sauce and add it to the pan. Stir-fry to combine and heat through, about 1 minute longer. Taste and adjust the seasonings, transfer to a warmed platter, and serve.

CHICKEN FAJITAS WITH CABBAGE SLAW

serves 4

Bursting with vitamin C, cabbage is a healthy and novel new replacement for traditional onion-and-pepper fajitas. The cabbage slaw can be made one day ahead of time. If you have it on hand, you can replace the chicken with lean steak or mahi mahi. Leftovers can be easily reheated and enjoyed again another night.

4 Tbsp (2 fl oz/60 ml) olive oil, plus more as needed

2 tsp chili powder

1 tsp crumbled dried oregano

1¼ lb (625 g) skinless, boneless chicken breasts, cut crosswise into ½-inch (12-mm) slices

2 large red onions, halved, and sliced lengthwise

Salt and freshly ground pepper

8–12 small corn tortillas

½ small head savoy cabbage, halved, cored, and thinly sliced

¼ cup (⅓ oz/10 g) chopped fresh cilantro

2 Tbsp fresh lime juice

1 large avocado, pitted, peeled, and sliced

In a large bowl, combine 2 Tbsp of the oil, the chili powder, and oregano. Add the chicken and onions and toss to coat. Season lightly with salt and pepper. Set aside.

Preheat the oven to 350°F (180°C). Wrap the tortillas in foil and place in the oven until heated through, about 15 minutes.

In another large bowl, combine the cabbage and cilantro. Add the remaining 2 Tbsp oil and toss to coat. Add the lime juice and toss well. Season to taste with salt and pepper, then transfer to a serving bowl. Arrange the avocado slices in a small bowl.

Warm 2 large frying pans over medium-high heat and brush with oil. Spread the chicken and onions in the pans and cook, turning occasionally with tongs, until the chicken is cooked through, about 5 minutes, and the onions are browned, about 7 minutes.

Transfer the chicken and onions to a warmed platter. Serve with the warm tortillas, cabbage slaw, and avocado slices, allowing diners to fill tortillas with their desired fillings.

WHOLE WHEAT FETTUCCINE WITH CHARD & GORGONZOLA

serves 4

Simple, yet comforting, this pasta dish features whole-wheat fettuccine and deep-green chard for optimum nutrients. Just a small amount of melted Gorgonzola goes a long way to bring richness to this meal.

5 Tbsp (3 fl oz/80 ml) olive oil

2 cloves garlic, minced

¾ lb (375 g) Swiss chard, ribs removed, leaves cut crosswise into thin strips

¾ cup (6 fl oz/180 ml) low-sodium chicken broth

Salt and freshly ground pepper

¾ lb (375 g) whole wheat fettuccine or linguine

¼ lb (125 g) mild Gorgonzola cheese, crumbled

Bring a large pot of water to a boil. In a large frying pan over medium heat, warm 1 tablespoon of the oil. Add the garlic and sauté until fragrant, about 1 minute. Add the chard and broth, cover, reduce the heat to medium-low, and cook, stirring occasionally, until the chard is wilted and the flavors have melded, about 7 minutes.

Meanwhile, add 2 Tbsp salt and the pasta to the boiling water. Cook, stirring occasionally to prevent sticking, until al dente, according to the package directions. Drain and add the pasta to the chard. Add the remaining 4 Tbsp (2 fl oz/60 ml) olive oil and the Gorgonzola and toss to combine. Warm briefly over low heat to melt the Gorgonzola and blend the flavors. Season with salt and pepper, and serve.

BLACK-EYED PEAS WITH SPICY YOGURT SAUCE

serves 6

This Indian-inspired dish is full of fresh, healthful ingredients like ginger, ripe tomatoes, and yogurt. It all comes together for a filling, protein-packed vegetarian dish that pairs well with steamed brown basmati rice.

1½ cups (10½ oz/330 g) dried black-eyed peas

¼ cup (2 fl oz/60 ml) olive oil

2 yellow onions, minced

¼ cup (1 oz/30 g) minced fresh ginger

6 cloves garlic, minced

1 tsp ground coriander

¾ tsp ground cumin

¼ tsp ground cardamom

2 ripe tomatoes, chopped

½ cup (4 oz/125 g) plain yogurt

¼ tsp cayenne pepper

Salt

¼ cup (⅓ oz/10 g) chopped fresh cilantro

Pick over the peas and discard any broken peas or grit. Rinse the peas well, place in a bowl, add water to cover by 2 inches (5 cm), and soak overnight.

Drain the peas and place in a saucepan with water to cover by 2 inches (5 cm). Bring to a boil, reduce the heat to low, and simmer, uncovered, until almost tender, about 35 minutes. Drain the peas, reserving the liquid. Set aside.

In a large frying pan over low heat, warm the oil. Add the onions and sauté until soft, about 10 minutes. Add the ginger, garlic, coriander, cumin, and cardamom and cook, stirring, for 2 minutes. Add the tomatoes, cover the pan, and cook for 2 minutes longer. Uncover and raise the heat to medium. Add 1 Tbsp of the yogurt and stir until fully incorporated into the sauce. Continue in the same manner with the remaining yogurt, adding 1 Tbsp at a time.

Add the reserved peas, ½ cup (4 fl oz/ 125 ml) of the cooking liquid, and the cayenne pepper and season with salt. Cover the pan and simmer over medium heat for 15 minutes. Uncover and continue to cook, stirring occasionally, until the liquid is very thick, 3–5 minutes.

Transfer the pea mixture to a warmed platter, garnish with the cilantro, and serve.

30

SPICY & SMOKY BUFFALO CHILI

serves 4–6

1 Tbsp olive oil

2 red bell peppers, cut
into ¾-inch (2-cm) pieces

1 large yellow onion, chopped

1 lb (500 g) ground bison (buffalo) or
ground beef

Salt and freshly ground pepper

2 tsp chipotle chile powder

1 tsp ground cumin

¼ tsp ground cinnamon

⅛ tsp ground cloves

2 cans (14½ oz/455 g each) diced tomatoes,
juices reserved

2 cans (15 oz/470 g each) pinto or
kidney beans, drained and rinsed

1 tsp dried oregano

1 cup (8 oz/250 g) plain yogurt (optional)

2 tsp grated lime zest (optional)

Look for ground bison, also called buffalo, at farmers markets or natural food stores. The meat is lower in saturated fat and higher in omega-3s than beef, but still has a rich, meaty flavor. Ground beef or turkey can replace the bison. Accompany with corn bread or corn tortillas.

In a large, heavy pot over medium-high heat, warm the oil. Add the peppers and onion and sauté until tender, about 10 minutes. Raise the heat to high, add the ground meat, and season with salt and pepper. Cook just until no longer red, breaking up the meat with a spoon, about 3 minutes. Add the chile, cumin, cinnamon, and cloves, and stir until fragrant, about 2 minutes. Add the tomatoes with their juices, the beans, oregano, and 1 cup (8 fl oz/250 ml) water. Cover and bring to a boil. Reduce the heat to medium-low and simmer until the flavors are blended, about 30 minutes.

Meanwhile, stir together the yogurt and lime zest in a small bowl, if using.

Taste the chili and adjust the seasoning. Spoon into warmed bowls with a dollop of lime-yogurt on top of each serving, if using, and serve.

31

ANGEL HAIR PASTA WITH SPRING VEGETABLES

serves 6

2 lb (1 kg) fava beans, shelled

Salt and freshly ground pepper

1 bunch baby carrots (about 6 oz/185 g),
trimmed, peeled, and halved lengthwise

½ lb (250 g) asparagus, tough ends removed,
cut into 2-inch (5-cm) lengths

½ lb (250 g) sugar snap peas, trimmed

6 tablespoons (3 fl oz/90 ml) olive oil

1 yellow onion, diced

3 cups (24 fl oz/750 ml) low-sodium
vegetable broth

1 lb (500 g) angel hair pasta

½ pint (6 oz/185 g) yellow pear tomatoes,
halved lengthwise

½ cup (½ oz/15 g) fresh basil leaves,
cut into slivers

2 oz (60 g) Parmesan cheese, shaved
with a vegetable peeler, or grated

We took the best of spring vegetables and let their natural flavors shine in this simple dish. An assortment of vegetables brings color and nutrients to this meal. A shower of fresh basil and Parmesan cheese lends bright flavors, replacing a heavy sauce.

Bring a saucepan three-fourths full of water to a boil and add the favas. Boil for 1 minute, then use a skimmer to transfer them to a bowl. Squeeze each bean free of its tough outer skin.

Lightly salt the boiling water. Add the carrots, boil for 2 minutes, and transfer to a bowl of ice water to stop the cooking. Repeat with the asparagus, blanching for 1 minute, and the snap peas, blanching for 30 seconds.

Bring a large pot three-fourths full of salted water to a rolling boil. Meanwhile, in a large sauté pan over medium heat, warm 3 Tbsp of the oil. Add the onion and sauté until golden, 5–7 minutes. Add the broth and boil until reduced by half, 10–15 minutes. Add the carrots, asparagus, snap peas, and fava beans. Heat until the vegetables are warmed through and just tender, 3–4 minutes. Season with salt and pepper.

When the water is boiling, stir in the pasta, and cook until al dente, 3–4 minutes or according to package directions. Drain and transfer to a warmed bowl. Toss with the remaining 3 Tbsp olive oil. Add the pasta to the pan with the vegetables and toss well. Transfer to a warmed serving bowl and scatter the tomatoes and basil on top. Sprinkle with the Parmesan, and serve.

April is the month for green vegetables: artichokes, peas, fava beans, and more asparagus appear at the market. Peas are a bright, fibrous addition to any meal—they sit pretty in a dainty pasta and morel dish and add a pop of color and nutrients alongside grilled lamb chops. The brisk weather is a great time to pull out the grill and start making healthy recipes outdoors. Newly budding spring herbs, such as dill and chives, make bright, seasonal garnishes.

1
PORK TENDERLOIN WITH RHUBARB CHUTNEY
page 80

2
PASTA WITH ENGLISH PEAS & MORELS
page 80

3
ASPARAGUS, PEA & FAVA BEAN STEW
page 83

8
PAN-SEARED CHICKEN WITH LENTIL & RADISH SALAD
page 85

9
ARTICHOKE-LEMON RAVIOLI
page 86

10
THAI RED CURRY BEEF
page 86

15
GRILLED LAMB CHOPS WITH PEA, FETA & MINT SALAD
page 91

16
SPAGHETTI CARBONARA WITH BLACK KALE
page 91

17
MISO-VEGETABLE NOODLE SOUP
page 92

22
TOFU & KALE WITH COCONUT-PEANUT SAUCE
page 95

23
SAUTÉED SCALLOPS & CHARD WITH LEMON-TARRAGON SAUCE
page 97

24
FAVA BEAN & RICOTTA OMELET W SPRING GREENS
page 97

29
CHICKEN TACOS WITH RADISH SLAW
page 101

30
ROASTED ASPARAGUS FARROTTO
page 101

april

1

Rhubarb is a stalky, tart fruit which becomes sweet and tender after cooking. It's important to remove any leaves and green parts of the rhubarb, which can be poisonous. All that should remain is the crimson shaft of the plant, which is rich in vitamin C and fiber. This sweet fruit-and-nut chutney compliments juicy pork tenderloin, which is a versatile, lean choice for any meal.

PORK TENDERLOIN WITH RHUBARB CHUTNEY

serves 4

FOR THE RHUBARB CHUTNEY

1 cup (7 oz/220 g) light brown sugar

½ cup (4 fl oz/125 ml) cider vinegar

1 Tbsp grated lemon zest

4 rhubarb stalks, cut into 1-inch (2.5-cm) pieces

1 cinnamon stick

2 Tbsp minced fresh ginger

½ cup (3 oz/90 g) golden raisins

¼ cup (1 oz/30 g) chopped walnuts

Salt and freshly ground pepper

1 pork tenderloin, about 1 lb (500 g)

Salt and freshly ground pepper

To make the chutney, in a nonreactive saucepan over low heat, cook the sugar, vinegar, and lemon zest, stirring until the sugar dissolves, about 5 minutes. Add the rhubarb, cinnamon stick, and ginger. Raise the heat to medium and cook, stirring often, until the rhubarb is soft, about 15 minutes. Remove the cinnamon stick. Add the raisins, walnuts, and a large pinch of salt and cook for about 3 minutes. Remove from the heat and set aside to cool.

Preheat the oven to 425°F (220°C). Line a small roasting pan with aluminum foil. Oil a flat roasting rack and place it in the pan.

Season the pork with salt and pepper. Roast the pork on the rack until a thermometer inserted into the thickest part registers 140°F (60°C) for medium, about 40 minutes. Remove from the oven, transfer the pork to a carving board, tent with foil, and let rest for 15 minutes.

Cut the pork into slices ½ inch (12 mm) thick. Arrange on a warmed platter, top with the chutney, and serve.

2

This dish features many small elements, each bursting with health benefits. Dainty English peas should be kept in their shells until just before cooking time, to retain freshness and vitamins. If meaty morels are not available, substitute cremini or shiitake mushrooms—all three varieties are equally potent in cancer-fighting selenium. Aromatic basil and a light dusting of Parmesan complete this light, springy meal.

PASTA WITH ENGLISH PEAS & MORELS

serves 4

Salt and freshly ground pepper

8 oz (250 g) ditalini or other small tube pasta

2 Tbsp olive oil

4 oz (125 g) morel mushrooms, halved lengthwise

4 cloves garlic, chopped

½ cup (4 fl oz/125 ml) low-sodium chicken or vegetable broth

½ cup (2½ oz/75 g) shelled English peas (about ½ lb/250 g unshelled)

4 Tbsp grated Parmesan cheese

1 lemon, zested

2 Tbsp chopped fresh basil leaves

Bring a pot of water to a boil over medium-high heat. Add ½ tsp salt and the ditalini and cook until al dente, about 10 minutes. Drain, reserving 1 cup (8 fl oz/250 ml) of the pasta water, and set aside.

Warm the oil in a large frying pan over medium-high heat. Add the mushrooms and garlic and season with salt and pepper. Sauté until the mushrooms absorb the oil, about 5 minutes. Add the broth and cook until the liquid is reduced by half, about 2 minutes. Add the peas and cook just until tender, about 3 minutes. Add the pasta to the pan along with ½ cup (4 fl oz/125 ml) of the reserved pasta water, 3 Tbsp of the Parmesan, the lemon zest, and 1 Tbsp basil. Stir to combine. Add additional pasta water if needed to achieve the desired consistency. Season with salt and pepper.

Transfer the contents of the pan to a serving bowl or individual plates, sprinkle with the remaining Parmesan and basil, and serve.

3

ASPARAGUS, PEA & FAVA BEAN STEW

serves 4–6

1 lb (500 g) fava beans, shelled

4 Tbsp (2 oz/60 g) unsalted butter

1 small leek, white and tender green parts only, sliced

3 cloves garlic, minced

1 cup (8 fl oz/250 ml) low-sodium chicken broth

1 cup (8 fl oz/250 ml) dry white wine

1 lb (500 g) English peas, shelled

1 lb (500 g) asparagus, trimmed and cut into 1½-inch pieces

1 cup (2 oz/60 g) torn pea shoots

1 Tbsp chopped fresh mint

1 Tbsp chopped fresh basil

1 Tbsp chopped fresh chives

1½ tsp finely grated lemon zest

Salt and freshly ground pepper

This lively stew is bursting with seasonal flavors. Green vegetables, beans, shelled peas, and fresh herbs make up this highly nutritious green meal. Stir cooked brown rice or barley into the stew for a more filling dish.

Bring a saucepan three-fourths full of water to a boil and add the favas. Boil for 1 minute, then drain. Squeeze each bean free of its tough outer skin.

In a large sauté pan, melt the butter over medium-high heat. Add the leek and sauté until soft, about 1 minute. Add the garlic and sauté for 30 seconds longer. Stir in the broth and wine and bring to a boil. Add the peas and asparagus and return to a boil. Reduce the heat to medium-low and simmer for 5 minutes. Using a slotted spoon, transfer the peas and asparagus to a warmed serving bowl. Raise the heat to medium high and simmer the liquid in the pan until reduced by about three-fourths, about 5 minutes.

Add the fava beans, pea shoots, mint, basil, and chives to the bowl with the peas and asparagus and toss to mix thoroughly. Pour the hot liquid in the pan over the vegetables and toss again. Stir in the lemon zest, season with salt and pepper, and serve.

4

SALMON SATAY BURGERS WITH CUCUMBER-ONION RELISH

serves 4

FOR THE CUCUMBER-ONION RELISH

1 cucumber, peeled and cut into ¼-inch (6-mm) dice

½ small red onion, quartered and thinly sliced

3 Tbsp rice wine vinegar

1 tsp sugar

¼ tsp salt

FOR THE SALMON SATAY BURGERS

1 lb (500 g) salmon, finely chopped

2 Tbsp finely chopped shallot

1 jalapeño chile, seeds and ribs removed, then finely chopped

1 stalk lemongrass, tender inner parts only, finely chopped

2 Tbsp chopped fresh cilantro

2 tsp ground cumin

2 tsp ground coriander

1 tsp ground turmeric

1 egg, slightly beaten

5 Tbsp whole-wheat panko bread crumbs

Salt and freshly ground pepper

Nonstick cooking spray

4 whole-wheat buns

Satay is an Indonesian dish of grilled and skewered meat or fish. The distinct flavors of the dish, such as lemongrass, cumin, and turmeric, help bring new life to traditional salmon burgers. Omega-3-packed salmon and whole-wheat panko bread crumbs make these burgers a healthy choice. Cucumbers and onions make a virtually calorie-free topping, while providing some great anti-inflammatory benefits.

To make the relish, in a bowl, combine the cucumber, onion, vinegar, sugar, and salt and stir well. Let stand at room temperature for 30 minutes, stirring occasionally.

In a large bowl, stir together the salmon, shallot, jalapeño, lemongrass, cilantro, cumin, coriander, and turmeric. Add the egg and the panko and mix well. Season with salt and pepper and form into 4 patties.

Heat a stove-top grill pan over medium-high heat and lightly coat it with cooking spray. Grill the patties until cooked through and golden-brown, about 4 minutes per side.

Divide the patties among the buns, top generously with the relish, and serve.

5

STUFFED ARTICHOKES WITH TUNA & BREAD CRUMBS

serves 4

After tasting fresh garlic bread crumbs, you may never want to go back to the store-bought version; these are made with whole-wheat bread for extra fiber and nutrients. Artichokes serve as an edible bowl and are full of liver-detoxifying compounds that are rarely found in other foods.

FOR THE BREAD CRUMBS

2 slices crusty country whole-wheat sourdough bread

1 clove garlic

2 cans (6 oz/185 g each) oil-packed tuna

½ cup (2 oz/60 g) grated Parmesan cheese

6 Tbsp (3 fl oz/90 ml) lemon juice

1½ Tbsp chopped fresh dill

Salt and freshly ground pepper

4 large artichokes

To make the bread crumbs, preheat the oven to 300°F (150°C). Place the bread on a baking sheet and bake, turning once, until lightly toasted, about 15 minutes. Rub 1 side of each slice with the garlic clove. Tear the bread into chunks and put in a food processor. Process until coarse crumbs form, then pour into a bowl. Increase the oven heat to 400°F (200°C).

Drain the tuna, reserving 2 Tbsp oil. Reserve ¼ cup (1 oz/30 g) of the bread crumbs. In a bowl, mix the remaining bread crumbs with the tuna, the reserved tuna oil, the cheese, 2 Tbsp lemon juice, dill, ¼ tsp salt, and ¼ tsp pepper.

Bring a pot of salted water to a boil and add the remaining 4 Tbsp (2 fl oz/60 ml) lemon juice. Cut about 1 inch (2.5 cm) off the top of each artichoke, then snip off any remaining thorny tips with shears. Break off the tough outer leaves, and use a vegetable peeler to peel the stems. Trim off the stem ends. Cook the artichokes in the water until the bases are tender when pierced with a knife, about 20 minutes. Remove with tongs and set aside, upside down, to drain and cool.

When cool enough to handle, scoop out the prickly chokes from the artichoke centers using a sturdy spoon. Cut off the stems, chop, and stir into the tuna mixture. Spread the leaves of each artichoke slightly and place upright in a baking dish. Spoon the tuna mixture evenly into artichoke centers and top evenly with the reserved bread crumbs. Bake, uncovered, until the crumbs are golden, 15–20 minutes, and serve.

6

SPINACH, HERB & SWISS CHEESE FRITTATA

serves 4–6

This one-pan dish teems with protein, vitamins, and fresh herbs. Serve it with crusty whole-wheat toast and a green salad for a complete healthy meal.

8 large eggs

¾ cup (3 oz/90 g) shredded Emmentaler cheese

Salt and freshly ground pepper

2 Tbsp olive oil

1 shallot, finely chopped

1 Tbsp chopped fresh basil

1 Tbsp chopped fresh thyme

1 Tbsp chopped fresh flat-leaf parsley

10 oz (315 g) baby spinach

Preheat the broiler. In a bowl, lightly whisk together the eggs and ½ cup (3 oz/90 g) of the cheese. Season lightly with salt and pepper and set aside.

In a well-seasoned 10-inch (25-cm) cast-iron frying pan, warm the oil over medium-high heat. Add the shallot and sauté until fragrant, about 2 minutes. Add the basil, thyme, and parsley and sauté for 30 seconds. Add the spinach and cook, stirring, until completely wilted, about 2 minutes.

Pour the egg mixture into the pan. Reduce the heat to medium-low and cook, without disturbing the egg mixture and adjusting the heat as needed to prevent the bottom from burning, until the frittata is set around the edges, 5–10 minutes.

Sprinkle the remaining ¼ cup (1 oz/30 g) cheese evenly over the top. Transfer the pan to the broiler and cook until the frittata is nearly set in the center and golden-brown on top, about 4 minutes, watching carefully to prevent burning. Let the frittata stand or at least 10 minutes or until cooled to room temperature. Cut into wedges and serve.

7

SPRING VEGETABLES WITH GINGER, LEMON & MINT

serves 4–6

1 lb (500 g) asparagus spears, ends trimmed and any thick stalks peeled

⅓ lb (155 g) sugar snap peas, trimmed

¼ lb (125 g) snow peas, trimmed

2 green onions, thinly sliced on the diagonal

1½ Tbsp minced peeled fresh ginger

1 Tbsp finely grated lemon zest

12 leaves fresh mint, cut into thin slivers, plus small leaves for garnish

2 Tbsp peanut or grapeseed oil

¾ tsp salt

Low-sodium soy sauce for seasoning (optional)

Fresh spring vegetables at the peak of their season need little adornment. Here, we stir-fry them quickly and flavor them with ginger and fresh mint, which contribute to digestive health, and lemon zest, which has cancer-fighting properties, for a surprising East-West twist on wok-style cooking.

Put the asparagus, sugar snaps, and snow peas in separate bowls near the stove. In 2 other small bowls, put the green onions and ginger. Add the lemon zest and mint to the bowl with the green onions.

Place a large wok on the stove top over high heat and let it warm for a minute or two. Swirl in the oil. Add the asparagus and ½ tsp of the salt and stir-fry for about 1 minute. Add the ginger and sugar snap peas and stir-fry for another minute. Add the snow peas and the remaining ¼ tsp salt and stir-fry until the snow peas are bright green and tender on the outside but still slightly crisp in the center, about 30 seconds longer. Add the green onions, lemon zest, and mint and toss briefly. Remove from the heat.

Adjust the seasonings, adding a little more salt or soy sauce. Transfer the vegetables to a warmed serving bowl or platter, garnish with the mint leaves, and serve.

8

PAN-SEARED CHICKEN WITH LENTIL & RADISH SALAD

serves 4

1 cup (7 oz/220 g) brown lentils, picked over and rinsed

1 small red onion, halved

1 bay leaf

Salt and freshly ground pepper

2 Tbsp red wine vinegar, plus 1 tsp

2 large celery stalks, finely chopped

1 large bunch radishes, trimmed, quartered lengthwise, and sliced

7 Tbsp (⅔ oz/20 g) fresh mint, minced

3 Tbsp Dijon mustard

6 Tbsp (3 fl oz/80 ml) extra-virgin olive oil

4 boneless, skinless chicken breast halves, about 6 oz (185 g) each, pounded to an even thickness

All-purpose flour, for dredging

Lentils and lean chicken pack protein into this French-inspired dish. Radishes are high in vitamin C and minerals, and their peppery bite lends freshness to the otherwise simple salad. The salad can be made one day ahead and chilled, or you can double it and serve the leftovers the next night.

Place the lentils in a saucepan, adding enough water to cover by 2 inches (5 cm). Add 1 onion half and the bay leaf, and bring to a boil. Reduce the heat, cover partially, and simmer until the lentils are just tender, about 30 minutes. Remove from the heat and stir in 2 tsp salt and 1 tsp vinegar. Drain the lentils and transfer to a medium bowl, remove and discard the onion and bay leaf. Finely chop the remaining onion. Mix the onion, celery, radishes, and 3 Tbsp mint into the lentils.

In a small bowl, whisk together the mustard and the remaining 2 Tbsp vinegar. Gradually whisk in 4 Tbsp (2 fl oz/60 ml) oil. Mix in the remaining 4 Tbsp mint and season with salt and pepper to make a dressing. Set aside 3 Tbsp of the dressing. Mix the remaining dressing into the lentil mixture.

Season the chicken with salt and pepper. Spread the flour on another plate. Dredge the chicken in the flour, shaking off the excess. In 2 large nonstick frying pans over medium-high heat, warm 1 Tbsp oil in each. Sauté 2 chicken breast halves in each pan until browned and cooked through, 4–5 minutes per side.

Slice the chicken, transfer to warmed plates, and spoon the lentil salad alongside. Drizzle with the reserved dressing, and serve.

9

Fluffy ricotta-and-artichoke-stuffed ravioli sit in a pool of light, fragrant vegetable broth, which melts the freshly grated Parmesan for a savory sauce. Topped with pea shoots, it makes an elegant spring dish.

ARTICHOKE-LEMON RAVIOLI

serves 4

Grated zest of 2 lemons, plus juice of 1 lemon

3 artichokes

Salt and freshly ground pepper

2 Tbsp olive oil

1 small yellow onion, chopped

4 cloves garlic, minced

¼ cup (2 oz/60 g) ricotta cheese

3 Tbsp freshly grated Parmesan cheese, plus more for garnish

1 Tbsp chopped fresh flat-leaf parsley

2 eggs

48 wonton wrappers (about 1 package)

Nonstick cooking spray

4 cups (32 fl oz/1 l) low-sodium chicken broth

1 cup (1 oz/30 g) pea shoots

Have ready a bowl of water to which you have added the lemon juice. Working with 1 artichoke at a time, pull off and discard the tough outer leaves until you reach the tender inner leaves. Cut off the stem and about 1 inch (2.5 cm) from the top to remove the prickly tips. Cut the trimmed artichokes lengthwise in quarters. As each artichoke is finished, drop it into the lemon water.

Bring a large saucepan of water to a boil over medium-high heat. Add the artichokes and 1 tsp salt. Cook until the artichokes are tender, about 20 minutes. Drain and transfer to a food processor. In a small frying pan over medium heat, warm 1 Tbsp of the oil. Add half each of the onion and garlic and sauté until softened, about 5 minutes. Transfer to the food processor. Pulse to finely chop the ingredients, then add the ricotta, Parmesan, parsley, 1 egg, and zest of 1 lemon. Season with salt and pepper and process until smooth.

In a small bowl, whisk together the remaining egg with 1 tsp water. On a work surface, lay a wonton wrapper and brush the surface with egg. Place 1 Tbsp of the filling in the center of the wrapper. Cover with a second wrapper, gently pushing out any air. Using a 3-inch (7.5-cm) round cutter, cut the ravioli into a round. Repeat using all the wonton wrappers and filling. ⟫→

Bring a saucepan of water to a boil over medium heat. Add 1 tsp salt and 3 or 4 ravioli at a time. Simmer gently until the pasta is just tender, about 2 minutes. Transfer to a baking sheet that has been lightly sprayed with nonstick cooking spray and continue to cook the remaining ravioli.

Warm the remaining 1 Tbsp oil in a saucepan over medium-high heat. Add the remaining onion and garlic and sauté until softened, about 5 minutes. Add the broth and the remaining lemon zest. Reduce the heat to low and simmer for 15 minutes. Season with salt and pepper. Divide the ravioli among bowls. Ladle the hot broth over the ravioli, garnish with pea shoots and Parmesan, and serve.

10

This classic Thai-style curry is full of healthy fats from coconut milk, beef, and peanuts to keep you satisfied. Choose grass-fed over corn-fed beef for increased nutrients. Have hot cooked brown rice on hand to serve with the curry.

THAI RED CURRY BEEF

serves 8

1 cup (8 fl oz/250 ml) unsweetened coconut milk

Juice of ½ lime

¼ cup (2 fl oz/60 ml) Asian fish sauce

2 tsp firmly packed golden brown sugar

4 Tbsp (2 fl oz/60 ml) canola or peanut oil

1 yellow onion, thinly sliced

1 red bell pepper, seeded and thinly sliced

1 Tbsp Thai red curry paste

1 lb (500 g) beef sirloin or tenderloin, cut against the grain into thin, bite-sized strips

2 Tbsp peanuts, toasted and chopped

¼ cup (⅓ oz/10 g) slivered fresh Thai basil

Stir together the coconut milk, lime juice, fish sauce, and brown sugar. Warm a wok over medium-high heat until hot and add 2 Tbsp of the oil. Add the onion and bell pepper and stir-fry just until tender, about 3 minutes. Transfer to a bowl. Add the remaining 2 Tbsp oil and the curry paste to the wok and stir-fry for 1 minute. Stir in the coconut milk mixture, bring to a gentle boil, and cook until the sauce begins to thicken, 5–7 minutes. Return the vegetables to the wok, stir in the beef, and simmer just until the beef is cooked through, about 2 minutes.

Transfer the curry to a serving bowl, garnish with the peanuts and basil, and serve.

LEMONGRASS-CHICKEN & VEGETABLE SOUP

serves 4

Fresh lemongrass, ginger, and chile add zing to a simple chicken soup. Noodles are swapped for squash, which is full of healthy carbohydrates. A bright garnish of cilantro and lime finish this Asian-inspired soup.

1 stalk lemongrass, trimmed, halved lengthwise, and smashed

½-inch (12-mm) piece fresh ginger, cut into 2 or 3 slices and smashed

1 Thai or serrano chile, cut into thin rounds

4 cups (32 fl oz/1 l) low-sodium chicken broth

2 Tbsp low-sodium soy sauce

1 shallot, minced

2 cloves garlic, minced

4 bone-in, skin-on chicken breast halves, (about 6 oz/185 g each)

Salt and freshly ground pepper

6 baby zucchini, cut in half on the diagonal

6 baby yellow squash, cut in half lengthwise

6 baby pattypan squash, cut in half pole to pole

6 baby carrots, cut in half lengthwise

Fresh cilantro sprigs for garnish

1 lime, cut into 8 wedges

In a large saucepan over high heat, combine the lemongrass, ginger, half of the chile, broth, soy sauce, shallot, and garlic, and bring to a simmer. Reduce the heat to low, cover, and simmer for 20 minutes. Meanwhile, season the chicken breast halves with ½ tsp salt and ¼ tsp pepper.

Add the chicken to the broth, raise the heat to medium-low, cover, and cook at a brisk simmer until the chicken shows no sign of pink when pierced with the tip of a sharp knife near the bone, about 30 minutes. Transfer the chicken to a large plate, keeping the broth covered and at a simmer. Remove and discard the skin and bones, then shred the chicken into bite-size pieces.

Remove and discard the lemongrass and ginger from the broth. Add the zucchini, yellow and pattypan squashes, carrots, and shredded chicken to the pan, cover, and continue to simmer until the vegetables are just tender, about 5 minutes. Taste the broth and adjust the seasonings.

Divide the soup evenly among warmed bowls and garnish with cilantro sprigs. Serve, passing the remaining chile slices, cilantro, and lime wedges at the table.

COUSCOUS VEGETABLE SALAD

serves 6

Couscous, a semolina pasta of tiny, round pellets that is a staple of North African cuisine, makes a great salad when tossed with a mixture of finely chopped, brightly colored vegetables. Other vegetables in season may be used; select them with contrasting flavors, textures, and colors in mind. Generally, the deeper the color of the vegetable (green, red, or orange), the higher the nutrient level.

1 cup (6 oz/185 g) whole-wheat couscous

Salt and freshly ground pepper

1½ cups (12 fl oz/375 ml) boiling water

3 Tbsp extra-virgin olive oil

3 Tbsp fresh lemon juice

1 clove garlic, minced

½ cup (2½ oz/75 g) thawed, frozen petite peas or blanched fresh petite peas

½ cup (1½ oz/45 g) thinly sliced green onion

½ cup (2½ oz/75 g) minced red bell pepper

½ cup (2½ oz/75 g) finely diced English cucumber

¼ cup (⅓ oz/10 g) finely chopped fresh flat-leaf parsley

1 cup (2 oz/60 g) firmly packed slivered romaine lettuce leaves

In a heatproof bowl, combine the couscous, ½ tsp salt, and the boiling water. Stir to blend. Cover tightly and let stand until all the liquid has been absorbed, about 20 minutes. Uncover and let cool to room temperature, about 15 minutes.

In a small bowl, whisk together the oil, lemon juice, garlic, ¼ tsp salt, 1 Tbsp water, and a grind of pepper until blended.

Add the peas, green onion, bell pepper, cucumber, parsley, and all but 1 Tbsp of the dressing to the couscous. Toss to mix. Place the romaine in a separate bowl. Add the remaining 1 Tbsp dressing and toss to coat.

Divide the lettuce evenly among individual bowls. Top each serving with the couscous mixture, and serve.

13

Here, ginger and watercress are blended with a variety of flavorful oils to form a pesto variation that is spread on the top of pink poached salmon. Pair this dish with roasted sweet potatoes for a super-nutritious and colorful meal.

POACHED SALMON WITH GINGER & WATERCRESS

serves 4

1 bunch watercress, stemmed

¼ cup (2 fl oz/60 ml) extra-virgin olive oil

¼ cup (2 fl oz/60 ml) grapeseed oil

2 tsp Asian sesame oil

2 Tbsp sesame seeds

Eight ¼-inch (6-mm) slices peeled fresh ginger

3 cloves garlic, thinly sliced

Grated zest of 1 lemon

Salt and freshly ground pepper

¼ cup (2 fl oz/60 ml) mirin

2 Tbsp fresh lemon juice

4 thick salmon fillets, each about 6 oz (185 g), skinned

In a food processor, combine the watercress, olive oil, grapeseed oil, sesame oil, sesame seeds, 2 slices of the ginger, one-third of the garlic, and the lemon zest and process until smooth and bright green. Season with salt and pepper.

In a large frying pan, heat 1 cup (8 fl oz/ 250 ml) water, the mirin, lemon juice, and remaining 6 slices of ginger over medium-high heat. When steam begins to rise from the liquid, reduce the heat to medium-low. Add the salmon fillets to the liquid and sprinkle lightly with salt. Cover the pan tightly and simmer until the salmon is barely opaque in the center, about 10 minutes. Remove from the heat and let stand, covered, for 5 minutes.

Transfer the salmon to a warmed platter, letting each fillet drain briefly. Spread 2 Tbsp of the watercress mixture on top of each fillet, and serve.

14

Soft poached eggs rest atop a bed of wilted chard and naturally creamy polenta for a delicious brunch or lunch. For the most nutrients, opt for stone-ground yellow polenta. If you like, sprinkle the dish with freshly grated Parmesan cheese just before serving.

POLENTA WITH CHARD & POACHED EGGS

serves 4

1 cup (5 oz/155 g) polenta

Salt and freshly ground pepper

2 bunches chard, about 2 lb (1 kg) total, stemmed and cut into 1-inch (2.5-cm) strips

2 Tbsp cider vinegar

8 very fresh large eggs

Freshly grated nutmeg

To make the polenta, in a large saucepan over high heat, bring 6 cups (48 fl oz/1.5 l) water and 1 tsp salt to a boil. Add the polenta in a slow, steady stream, stirring constantly. Reduce the heat to low and cook, stirring often, until the polenta pulls away from the sides of the pan, 40–45 minutes.

While the polenta is cooking, place the chard in a large sauté pan, sprinkle with a little salt, and add ¼ cup (2 fl oz/60 ml) water. Cover and set over medium-high heat. Cook the chard, stirring occasionally, until wilted and tender, about 10 minutes. Transfer to a colander and, using a spoon, press against the chard to remove all the liquid. Fluff up with a fork. Cover to keep warm.

To poach the eggs, pour water into a very large sauté pan to a depth of 1½ inches (4 cm). Add the vinegar and 1 tsp salt. Bring to a low simmer over medium heat. Break the eggs, one at a time, into a ramekin and ease each egg into the water. When the whites have firmed a little, spoon the water over the eggs and continue to cook until the whites are just set and the yolks are just glazed over but still liquid, 3–5 minutes.

To serve, divide the warm polenta among 4 warmed plates. Sprinkle with a little nutmeg. Top the polenta with the chard, dividing evenly. Using a slotted spoon, pick up the eggs, drain briefly on paper towels, and place 2 eggs on top of each portion of chard. Sprinkle the eggs with salt and pepper, and serve.

15

GRILLED LAMB CHOPS WITH PEA, FETA & MINT SALAD

serves 4

Lean lamb is a good source of protein and minerals. To ensure the best quality and most nutrients, look for grass-fed, pasture-raised lamb at the butcher shop. Thawed frozen peas can be used in place of fresh, and don't need to be blanched.

Grated zest of 1 lemon

2 Tbsp fresh lemon juice

2 large garlic cloves, minced

3 Tbsp olive oil

8 lamb chops, each 4–5 oz (125–155 g) and 1–1¼ inches (2.5–3 cm) thick

3 cups (15 oz/470 g) shelled English peas

Salt and freshly ground pepper

2 Tbsp minced fresh mint

1 Tbsp red wine vinegar

3 oz (90 g) feta cheese, crumbled

In a shallow nonreactive dish large enough to hold the chops in one layer, whisk together the lemon zest and juice, garlic, and 1 Tbsp of the oil. Add the lamb chops, turn to coat, and let stand for 30 minutes, turning once halfway through.

Have ready a bowl of ice water. Bring a pot of lightly salted water to a rapid boil. Add the peas and cook until not quite tender, 1–2 minutes. Immediately drain and transfer to the ice water to stop the cooking. Drain well and pat thoroughly dry.

In a bowl, combine the peas, the remaining 2 Tbsp oil, and the mint. Add ½ tsp salt and season with pepper. Toss gently.

Prepare a grill for direct-heat cooking over high heat. Pat the lamp chops dry with paper towels and season both sides generously with salt. Place on the grill rack and cook until dark brown and sizzling, 3–5 minutes. Turn over the chops and continue to cook for 3–5 more minutes for medium-rare, or to your desired doneness. Transfer to a platter, season with pepper, and let rest for 5–10 minutes.

Stir the vinegar and cheese into the pea salad. Serve alongside the chops.

16

SPAGHETTI CARBONARA WITH BLACK KALE

serves 2

This makes a great meal for two on a busy night. Double it to serve more. Black kale, also known as lacinato and dinosaur kale, adds nutrients and textural contrast to tender spaghetti. Excluding cream, cutting down the pancetta used, and using a multigrain pasta all help to keep this carbonara healthy. To prevent overcooking, which will cause curdling, take the frying pan off the heat before adding in the egg mixture. Then, only if necessary, cook over very low heat and stir constantly just until the eggs start to thicken.

2 oz (60 g) pancetta, chopped

1 large shallot, minced

¼ cup (2 fl oz/60 ml) dry white wine

Salt and freshly ground pepper

8 oz (250 g) dried spaghetti, preferably multigrain

1 bunch black kale, chopped

2 large eggs

¼ cup (1 oz/30 g) freshly grated Parmesan cheese

¼ cup (1 oz/30 g) freshly grated Romano cheese

Place a large frying pan over medium-high heat. Add the pancetta and sauté until beginning to brown, about 3 minutes. Add the shallot and sauté for 2 minutes. Add the wine and boil until reduced by half, stirring up the browned bits on the pan bottom, about 30 seconds. Remove the frying pan from the heat.

Bring a large pot of salted water to a boil. Add the spaghetti, stir well, and cook for 5 minutes. Add the kale and cook until the pasta is al dente, about 5 minutes more.

Meanwhile, in a small bowl, beat the eggs with a fork. Mix in both cheeses and a generous amount of pepper.

Reserve ½ cup (4 fl oz/125 ml) of the pasta cooking water. Drain the pasta. Reheat the pancetta mixture briefly, and then remove from the heat and add the spaghetti and kale to the frying pan. Gradually whisk ¼ cup (2 fl oz/60 ml) of the reserved pasta cooking liquid into the egg mixture. Add the egg mixture to the frying pan and stir until it coats the pasta and is creamy, not wet and runny. If the egg mixture does not become creamy, set the frying pan over very low heat and stir constantly just until it becomes creamy, watching carefully (do not boil). Immediately remove the frying pan from the heat. Mix in enough of the remaining ¼ cup pasta cooking liquid to form a silky texture.

Divide between 2 warmed bowls, and serve.

17

*Red miso is richer
in antioxidants
and other health
benefits than its
white counterpart.
Here it's used
among a handful
of simple ingredients
to allow the true
colors and flavors
of the vegetable-
and-noodle soup
to shine through.*

MISO-VEGETABLE NOODLE SOUP

serves 4

1 lb (500 g) udon noodles

4 cups (32 fl oz/1 l) low-sodium vegetable broth or stock

3 thin slices peeled fresh ginger

2 Tbsp sake

2 Tbsp red miso

¼ lb (125 g) silken tofu, cut into ½-inch (12-mm) cubes

2 large button mushrooms, thinly sliced

1 small carrot, thinly sliced

1 large green onion, dark green part only, thinly sliced lengthwise

Fill a large pot half full with water and bring to a boil over high heat. Add the noodles, return the water to a boil, and cook until the noodles are al dente, 2–3 minutes. Drain the noodles and rinse well under cold water. Divide among 4 soup bowls.

In a saucepan over medium-high heat, warm the broth with the ginger and sake until bubbles begin to form around the edge of the pan. Reduce the heat to medium-low and simmer for 5 minutes. Remove and discard the ginger. Place the miso in a small bowl and add ¼ cup (2 fl oz/60 ml) of the hot broth. Stir until the miso is dissolved and creamy, then pour into the pot.

Place the tofu in a sieve and warm it under a slow stream of hot running water. Divide the tofu among the soup bowls. Ladle in the hot broth, dividing it among the bowls. Garnish with the sliced mushroom, carrot, and green onion, and serve.

18

*Eating fish a few
times a week helps
ensure you are
getting heart healthy
omega-3s in your
diet. This recipe is
an easy blueprint
for preparing fish
any day of the week:
sear sustainable fish
fillets, serve them
over your favorite
vegetables simmered
in broth, top with
bacon for additional
flavor, and dinner
is served.*

HALIBUT WITH SPRING VEGETABLES

serves 4

2 Yukon gold potatoes, about 10 oz (315 g) total weight, peeled and cubed

1 package (10 oz/315 g) frozen artichoke hearts, thawed

1 leek, white part only, cut into thin slices

3 cloves garlic, thinly sliced

1¾ cups (14 fl oz/430 ml) low-sodium chicken broth

1 tsp fresh thyme leaves

1 dried bay leaf

Salt and freshly ground pepper

Pinch of red pepper flakes

2 slices thick-cut bacon, chopped

½ lb (250 g) cremini mushrooms, chopped

1 Tbsp *each* sherry vinegar and extra-virgin olive oil

1½ lb (750 g) skinless halibut fillets

2 tbsp minced fresh flat-leaf parsley

In a large saucepan, combine the potatoes, artichokes, leek, garlic, broth, thyme, bay leaf, ½ tsp salt, a few grinds of black pepper, and the pepper flakes and bring to a boil over medium-high heat. Reduce the heat to low, cover, and simmer until the vegetables are tender, 10–12 minutes.

In a frying pan over medium heat, sauté the bacon until crisp, 3–4 minutes. Transfer to paper towels. Add the mushrooms to the pan, season with salt and pepper, and sauté until tender and lightly browned, 3–4 minutes. Add the vinegar and cook for 1 minute. Remove from the heat.

Remove the vegetables from the heat and remove and discard the bay leaf. Stir in the mushrooms and cover to keep warm.

Warm a large frying pan over medium-high heat. Add the oil. Add the fillets and sear, turning once, until nicely browned and opaque throughout, about 8 minutes total. Transfer the fillets to a cutting board and cut into large, equal pieces.

Divide the vegetable mixture among warmed shallow soup bowls. Top each bowl with the halibut pieces, dividing evenly, garnish with the reserved bacon and the parsley, and serve.

19

PARCHMENT-BAKED CHICKEN WITH POTATOES & PEAS

serves 4

4 boneless, skinless chicken breast halves, about 6 oz (185 g) each

Salt and freshly ground pepper

1½ Tbsp unsalted butter, at room temperature

4 tsp Dijon mustard

2 tsp minced fresh tarragon

1 tsp minced shallot

4 small red potatoes, cut into ¼-inch (6-mm) rounds

¾ lb (375 g) English peas, shelled

4 Tbsp (2 fl oz/60 ml) dry white wine

This nearly fat-free dish is flavored by a slim pat of butter, lots of mustard, tarragon, and white wine to impart all the classic French flavors. Steamed together in parchment paper in the oven means that both serving and cleanup is a breeze. Serve the chicken and vegetables alongside a green salad.

Pound each chicken breast half until flattened to an even thickness of about ½ inch (12 mm). Season the chicken with 1 tsp salt and ½ tsp pepper. In a small bowl, mix together the butter, mustard, tarragon, and shallot. Season with salt and pepper.

Preheat the oven to 400°F (200°C). Bring a saucepan of lightly salted water to a boil over high heat. Add the potatoes and cook for 2 minutes. Add the peas, cook for 2 minutes longer, and then drain the vegetables well.

Cut 4 pieces of parchment paper, each about 12 by 18 inches (30 by 45 cm). Lay the pieces on a work surface. Put a chicken breast slightly off center on each piece of parchment. Layer the ingredients on top of the chicken: one-fourth of the butter, one-fourth of the potato-pea mixture, and 1 Tbsp of the wine. Season lightly with salt and pepper. Fold the parchment in half over the chicken by bringing the short sides together and folding them to seal. Fold in the sides so that none of the juices or steam can escape. Place the packets on a baking sheet and place in the oven. Bake until the paper begins to brown and puff, about 20 minutes. Remove from the oven and let stand for 5 minutes. To test for doneness, press the chicken with a fingertip through the paper. It should feel firm and spring back. Remove from the oven and let stand for 5 minutes.

Place the packets on warmed plates. Carefully slit an X in the top of each packet to let the steam escape, and serve.

20

BULGUR & LENTIL PILAF WITH ALMOND GREMOLATA

serves 4

¾ cup (5 oz/155 g) brown lentils, picked over, rinsed, and drained

2 Tbsp olive oil

1 yellow onion, chopped

2 cloves garlic, minced

1 cup (6 oz/185 g) bulgur

1 tsp ground coriander

Salt and freshly ground pepper

2 cups (16 fl oz/500 ml) low-sodium vegetable broth or water

½ cup (½ oz/15 g) fresh parsley leaves

¼ cup (1 oz/30 g) toasted almonds

1 Tbsp grated lemon zest

2 Tbsp lemon juice

Lentils, bulgur, and almonds create a dish that is complex in textures and bursting with protein. Serve this dish with a side of steamed broccoli for added color and nutrients. The gremolata lends a fresh, tangy flavor and crunchy texture to the dish.

In a small saucepan, cover the lentils with water and simmer until tender but firm to the bite, about 20 minutes. Drain.

In a large frying pan over medium-high heat, warm the oil. Add the onion and garlic and cook, stirring often, until translucent, 3–5 minutes. Stir in the bulgur, coriander, ¼ tsp salt, and ¼ tsp ground pepper. Cook for 1 minute. Stir in the lentils and broth and bring to a boil. Reduce the heat to low, cover, and simmer for 5 minutes. Remove from the heat and let stand, covered, for 15 minutes.

Coarsely chop the parsley, almonds, and lemon zest together on a cutting board. Fluff the pilaf with a fork and stir in the lemon juice. Season to taste with salt and pepper. To serve, spoon the pilaf onto a platter and sprinkle with the almond mixture.

21

BAKED SEA BASS WITH GARLIC & ARTICHOKES

serves 4

Here, braised artichokes soften and tenderize in an infused wine sauce. Firm sea bass fillets are then cooked directly on top of the artichokes for an easy one-pot meal. Serve this dish with wedges of lemon and roasted potatoes.

Juice of 1 lemon

16 small artichokes

3 Tbsp extra-virgin olive oil

1 clove garlic, minced

¼ cup (2 fl oz/60 ml) low-sodium chicken broth

3 Tbsp dry white wine

¼ cup (1½ oz/45 g) niçoise olives

1 tsp minced fresh thyme

1 tsp minced fresh flat-leaf parsley

½ tsp freshly ground pepper

4 sea bass fillets, each about ⅓ lb (155 g) and 1 inch (2.5 cm) thick

Preheat the oven to 400°F (200°C).

Have ready a large bowl of cold water to which you have added the lemon juice. Working with 1 artichoke at a time, snap off a few of the tough outer leaves until you reach the pale green inner leaves. Cut off a small piece from the stem end, and trim off the thorny leaf tops with a serrated knife. Depending on their size, cut the artichoke lengthwise in half or into 4 or 6 pieces. If necessary, using a small spoon, scoop out the fuzzy choke. As each artichoke is trimmed, drop it into the lemon water to prevent discoloration. When all of the artichokes have been trimmed, drain and pat dry with paper towels.

In a flameproof baking dish, warm the oil over medium heat. Add the garlic and artichokes and sauté until the artichokes begin to soften and turn golden, 5–6 minutes. Stir in the broth, wine, olives, thyme, parsley, and pepper. Add the sea bass in a single layer, spooning some of the sauce over the top. Cover, transfer to the oven, and bake until the base of an artichoke is easily pierced with a fork and the fish is opaque throughout, 15–20 minutes.

Serve from the baking dish or arrange on a warmed platter.

22

TOFU & KALE WITH COCONUT-PEANUT SAUCE

serves 4

Peanuts, tofu, and coconut milk are great sources of healthy-fats, omega-3s, and cancer-fighting antioxidants. Serve this dish with brown rice sprinkled with chopped spring onions.

½ cup (5 oz/155 g) creamy peanut butter

½ cup (4 fl oz/125 ml) unsweetened coconut milk

3 Tbsp fresh lime juice

2 Tbsp firmly packed brown sugar

2 Tbsp low-sodium soy sauce

2 tsp Sriracha sauce

About 1 lb (500 g) lacinato kale, stemmed and roughly chopped

1 lb (500 g) firm tofu, cut into 1-inch (2.5-cm) cubes

In a blender, combine the peanut butter, coconut milk, lime juice, brown sugar, soy sauce, and Sriracha sauce and process until smooth. Transfer the peanut sauce to a bowl and set aside.

Set a steamer rack inside a large pot filled with a couple inches of water. Place the kale in the rack and bring water to a boil over medium-high heat. Cover the pot and steam until the kale is wilted, about 7 minutes. Place the tofu on top of the kale. Cover and steam until the tofu is heated through, about 5 minutes more.

Divide the kale and tofu among warmed plates and serve, passing the peanut sauce at the table.

23

Scallops boast a neutral flavor and a plump, meaty texture. When dusted in a light flour coating, they develop a pleasing crisp crust. Try whole-wheat flour in place of all-purpose for a healthier choice. If you wish, the chard can be replaced by fresh spinach.

SAUTÉED SCALLOPS & CHARD WITH LEMON-TARRAGON SAUCE

serves 2

3 Tbsp olive oil

1 small bunch chard, stemmed and chopped

Salt and freshly ground pepper

¾ lb (375 g) sea scallops

All-purpose flour, for dredging

1 small shallot, minced

¼ cup (2 fl oz/60 ml) dry white wine

½ cup (4 fl oz/125 ml) low-sodium chicken broth

1 Tbsp fresh lemon juice

½ tsp Dijon mustard

½ tsp minced fresh tarragon, plus more for garnish

1 Tbsp unsalted butter (optional)

Cooked brown jasmine or basmati rice for serving

In a large nonstick frying pan over medium-high heat, warm 1 Tbsp of the oil. Add the chard, sprinkle lightly with salt and pepper, and sauté until just softened, about 3 minutes. Transfer to a bowl and cover to keep warm.

Sprinkle the scallops lightly with salt and pepper, and then dredge in flour. In the frying pan over medium-high heat, warm 1 Tbsp of the oil. Add the scallops and cook until springy to the touch and no longer translucent in the center, about 3 minutes on each side. Transfer the scallops to a plate. Add the remaining 1 Tbsp oil to the pan. Add the shallot and sauté until it begins to soften, about 1 minute. Add the wine and boil until almost evaporated, stirring up any browned bits on the pan bottom, about 2 minutes. Add the broth, lemon juice, mustard, and ½ tsp tarragon, and boil until slightly thickened, about 2 minutes. Remove from the heat and stir in the butter, if using. Season the sauce with salt and pepper.

Spoon rice into the center of 2 warmed plates, top with the chard and then the scallops. Spoon the sauce on top, garnish with minced tarragon and serve.

24

This springy dish is perfect as the star of a healthy brunch. Fava beans are low in fat and sodium and high in iron and fiber. Here they are enveloped in creamy, protein-packed eggs and smooth ricotta, for a meal that will satisfy your hunger.

FAVA BEAN & RICOTTA OMELET WITH SPRING GREENS

serves 4

2 lb (1 kg) fava beans, shelled

5 Tbsp (3 oz/90 g) part-skim ricotta cheese

¼ cup (¾ oz/20 g) chopped fresh basil

Grated zest and juice of 1 lemon

Salt and freshly ground pepper

8 large eggs

3 Tbsp olive oil

2 cups (2 oz/60 g) spring greens, such as arugula or watercress

Bring a saucepan three-fourths full of water to a boil and add the favas. Boil for 1 minute, then use a skimmer to transfer them to a bowl. Squeeze each bean free of its tough outer skin. Set aside ½ cup (3½ oz/105 g) of the fava beans and transfer the remaining beans to a food processor. Add the ricotta, basil, and lemon zest and process until smooth. Season to taste with salt and pepper.

Preheat the oven to 200°F (95°C). In a bowl, whisk the eggs with 1 Tbsp water until frothy. Season with salt and pepper.

Melt ½ Tbsp oil in a small nonstick frying pan over medium heat. Pour in one-fourth of the egg mixture. Cook until the eggs just begin to set, about 1 minute. Using a spatula, gently lift one side of the egg while tilting the pan to allow the uncooked egg mixture to drip to the bottom of the pan. Repeat until the egg is cooked through, about 3 minutes.

Place one-quarter of the puréed fava mixture onto half of the omelet and fold over the other side. Transfer to a plate and keep warm in the oven. Repeat the cooking process 3 more times.

Place the spring greens in a bowl. Drizzle with the remaining 1 Tbsp oil and the lemon juice and season with salt and pepper. Top each omelet with the remaining fava beans and the spring greens, dividing evenly, and serve.

25

*You won't find
any empty calories
in this healthy
risotto. Fiber-rich
barley is a smart
carbohydrate choice
because it helps
you feel full for
hours. Wilted
radicchio and
soft artichokes
are nutrient-rich
add-ins which
can be replaced by
your favorite leafy
green vegetable.*

ARTICHOKE & RADICCHIO BARLEY RISOTTO

serves 4

Juice of 1 lemon

16 baby artichokes, about 1 lb (500 g) total

1 Tbsp olive oil

¾ cup (3 oz/90 g) chopped yellow onion

1 cup (8 oz/250 g) pearl barley

3¼ cups (26 fl oz/810 ml) low-sodium vegetable broth

2 tsp chopped fresh thyme

1 cup (3 oz/90 g) thinly sliced radicchio

2 Tbsp grated Parmesan cheese, plus more for serving

Salt and freshly ground pepper

Have ready a large bowl of cold water to which you have added the lemon juice. Working with 1 artichoke at a time, snap off a few of the tough outer leaves until you reach the pale green inner leaves. Cut off a small piece from the stem end, and trim off the thorny leaf tops with a serrated knife. Depending on their size, cut the artichokes in half or quarters. If necessary, using a small spoon, scoop out the fuzzy choke. As each artichoke is trimmed, drop it into the lemon water to prevent discoloration. Bring a saucepan three-fourths full of water to a boil. Drain the artichokes and add them to the boiling water. Cook until tender when pierced with the tip of a knife, about 10 minutes. Drain well and set aside.

Warm a saucepan over medium heat and add the oil. Add the onion and sauté until softened, about 4 minutes. Add the barley and stir for 1 minute. Stir in 2 cups (16 fl oz/ 500 ml) of the broth and bring to a simmer. Simmer the barley, stirring frequently, for 10 minutes. Stir in the remaining 1¼ cups (10 fl oz/310 ml) broth and continue to simmer, stirring frequently, just until the barley is tender, about 15 minutes. Stir in the artichokes and thyme and heat through, about 2 minutes. Remove from the heat and stir in ⅔ cup (2 oz/60 g) of the radicchio and the 2 Tbsp cheese. Adjust the seasonings.

Divide the barley evenly among warmed serving bowls. Sprinkle with the remaining ⅓ cup (1 oz/30 g) radicchio and a little Parmesan cheese, dividing evenly, and serve.

26

*This protein-packed
dish is perfect to
serve to a crowd—
it's hearty and
large batches can
be made easily from
economical pantry
staples. It also keeps
well, so if you're
eating vegetarian,
make a big batch on
Sunday and save
the leftovers for
later in the week.*

CHICKPEA & POTATO CURRY

serves 4–6

2 Tbsp grapeseed oil

1½ cups (6 oz/185 g) thin yellow onion wedges

3 cloves garlic, pressed

3 Tbsp peeled, grated ginger

¾ tsp cumin seeds

2 cups (12 oz/375 g) canned or fresh diced tomatoes with their juice

2 tsp garam masala

½ tsp ground turmeric

½ tsp ground coriander

Salt

2 cups (10 oz/315 g) cubed Yukon gold potatoes

5 cups (35 oz/1 kg) canned chickpeas, rinsed and drained

¼ cup (⅓ oz/10 g) chopped fresh cilantro

2 Tbsp lime juice

Steamed brown basmati rice and plain yogurt for serving

Warm a large saucepan over medium-high heat and add the oil. Add the onion, garlic, and ginger, and sauté until the garlic starts to brown, 1–2 minutes. Add the cumin seeds, tomatoes, garam masala, turmeric, coriander, and 2 cups (16 fl oz/500 ml) water. Season with 1 tsp salt, and bring to a boil. Reduce the heat to medium-low and simmer, uncovered, for 15 minutes. Add the potatoes and chickpeas and continue to simmer until the potatoes are tender, 15–20 minutes more.

Season with salt and mix in the cilantro and lime juice. Transfer to a warmed serving bowl and serve, passing the rice and yogurt at the table.

27

TUNA BURGERS WITH CREAMY SMOKED PAPRIKA SAUCE

serves 4

1 lb (500 g) tuna steak, finely chopped

1 Tbsp Dijon mustard

¼ cup (⅓ oz/10 g) whole-wheat panko bread crumbs

1½ Tbsp chopped green onions

Salt and freshly ground pepper

FOR THE SMOKED PAPRIKA SAUCE

3 Tbsp olive oil mayonnaise

2 Tbsp plain yogurt

1 Tbsp fresh lemon juice

¼ tsp smoked paprika

Salt

Nonstick cooking spray

4 soft whole-grain rolls

These simple burgers come together in minutes and the raw patties can be made a day ahead of time. Use hot or sweet paprika to match your heat preference.

Put the tuna in a bowl and add the mustard, panko, and green onions. Stir to mix and season with salt and pepper. Shape the mixture into 4 patties and refrigerate for 30 minutes.

To make the sauce, mix together the mayonnaise, yogurt, lemon juice, and smoked paprika in a small bowl and season with salt.

Set a nonstick frying pan over medium-high heat and lightly coat with cooking spray. Fry the burgers until medium-rare, about 4 minutes per side. Serve the burgers on the rolls with the sauce.

28

UDON NOODLES WITH POACHED SHRIMP, BABY SPINACH & MISO

serves 6

Salt

8 cups (64 fl oz/2 l) low-sodium vegetable broth

4 thin slices fresh ginger

1 bunch green onions, thinly sliced, green tops and white bottoms separated

¼ bunch fresh cilantro, leaves coarsely chopped and stems reserved

¼ cup (2 oz/60 g) white miso

2 tsp low-sodium soy sauce

½ tsp Sriracha sauce

1 lb (500 g) medium shrimp, peeled and deveined

1 lb (500 g) udon noodles

3 cups (3 oz/90 g) baby spinach

Miso paste is full of antioxidants, known to help prevent cancer. Here it pairs with fresh ginger, bright cilantro, and spicy Sriracha sauce for a broth bursting with flavor and health benefits. The shrimp can be replaced by cooked, shredded chicken.

Bring a large pot of generously salted water to a boil over high heat.

In a medium saucepan, combine the broth, ginger, green onion tops, and cilantro stems. Bring the mixture to a boil over high heat, then reduce the heat to medium and let the broth simmer until the flavors are infused, 20–25 minutes.

Strain the broth and return it to the pan, discarding the solids. Return the pan to medium heat and whisk in the miso, soy sauce, and Sriracha sauce until smooth. Add the shrimp and cook, stirring occasionally, until they are just pink and opaque, 1–2 minutes.

When the water comes to a boil, add the udon and cook just until tender, 2–3 minutes. Drain the noodles well.

Divide the spinach among 6 shallow soup bowls. Top the spinach with the noodles and ladle the broth over the top, adding a few shrimp to each bowl. Garnish with the chopped cilantro and green onion bottoms, and serve.

29

Peppery and refreshing radishes are enhanced with green onion, cilantro, and lime juice for a fresh take on traditional salsa. Skinless chicken thighs are simmered in a spiced citrus juice until they barely fall apart, then shredded and folded into whole-grain corn tortillas for tacos.

CHICKEN TACOS WITH RADISH SLAW

serves 6

FOR THE CHICKEN

⅔ cup (5 fl oz/150 ml) fresh orange juice

3 Tbsp fresh lime juice

3 Tbsp achiote paste

1 small yellow onion, chopped

2 cloves garlic, chopped

½ tsp dried oregano

2 lb (1 kg) boneless, skinless chicken thighs

Salt and freshly ground pepper

12 small soft corn tortillas, each 4 inches (10 cm) in diameter

FOR THE RADISH SLAW

18 radishes, halved and thinly sliced

⅓ cup (½ oz/15 g) chopped fresh cilantro

2 green onions, thinly sliced

1 Tbsp fresh lime juice

2 large avocados, halved, pitted, and sliced

3 oz (90 g) cotija cheese, crumbled

To prepare the chicken, in a heavy Dutch oven, stir together the orange juice, lime juice, and achiote paste until smooth. Add the onion, garlic, and oregano and mix well. Add the chicken and turn to coat evenly. Sprinkle the chicken with salt. Cover the pot and place over medium heat. Bring to a simmer, then reduce the heat to low and cook, stirring occasionally, until the sauce has thickened and the chicken is opaque throughout, about 40 minutes Uncover and continue to simmer until the sauce is very thick and the chicken begins to fall apart about 10 minutes. Let the chicken cool slightly, then shred. Season with salt and pepper.

Wrap the tortillas in foil and seal tightly. Place in a warm oven for 10 minutes.

To make the slaw, in a small bowl, combine the radishes, cilantro, green onions and lime juice and toss to mix. Season with salt.

Arrange 2 tortillas on each individual plate. Top the tortillas with the chicken, dividing evenly, and spoon the radish slaw evenly over the chicken. Top with avocado slices and cheese, and serve.

30

Farrotto is farro that has been cooked in the style of risotto. Farro is a whole grain that has a much nuttier, crunchier consistency than Arborio rice used in traditional risotto. Rich in tension-relieving magnesium, farro makes a healthy replacement in this comfort food. Asparagus adds color and a hearty dose of fiber, but it can also be replaced with pumpkin in the fall or root vegetables in the winter.

ROASTED ASPARAGUS FARROTTO

serves 4–6

1 lb (500 g) asparagus, trimmed

2 Tbsp plus 1 tsp olive oil

⅛ tsp balsamic vinegar

Salt and freshly ground pepper

4½ cups (36 fl oz/1.1 l) low-sodium chicken broth

1 small yellow onion, chopped

3 cloves garlic, chopped

2 cups (14½ oz/455 g) farro, rinsed

½ cup (4 fl oz/125 ml) white wine

6 Tbsp (1½ oz/45 g) grated Parmesan cheese, plus more for serving

Preheat the oven to 400°F (200°C). Cut the asparagus into 1-inch (2.5-cm) pieces and toss with 1 tsp of the oil and the vinegar. Place in a single layer on a baking sheet and season with salt and pepper. Roast until fork-tender, about 8 minutes. Set aside.

Warm the broth in a small saucepan over low heat. In a medium saucepan over medium heat, warm the remaining 2 Tbsp oil. Add the onion and garlic and sauté until soft, about 5 minutes. Add the farro and stir to combine. Allow the farro to toast for 2 minutes, stirring several times. Add the wine and cook until all the liquid is absorbed, about 5 minutes.

Stir about 1 cup (8 fl oz/250 ml) of the broth into the farro and cook until the liquid is absorbed, about 5 minutes. Repeat this process until all the broth is incorporated and the farro is tender, about 20 minutes.

Remove the farro from the heat and stir in the reserved asparagus and the Parmesan. Season with salt and pepper and serve, passing additional cheese at the table.

April showers bring May vegetables. This is the time to replace stews and baked dishes with light salads and grilled poultry and fish. As the days get warmer, savor healthy meals in the outdoors, dining al fresco–style. Spring vegetables can be enjoyed in so many forms beyond a salad: they make flavorful additions atop a bed of creamy polenta, add texture to grilled pizzas, and bring beautiful color to roasted meats.

may

1

BRAISED ARTICHOKES WITH SHALLOTS & PEAS

serves 4–6

Finely grated zest and juice of 2 lemons

6 large artichokes, about ½ lb (250 g) each

3 Tbsp olive oil

2 large shallots, finely chopped

1 sprig fresh thyme

½ cup (4 fl oz/125 ml) dry white wine

1½ cups (12 fl oz/375 ml) low-sodium chicken broth, plus more if needed

Salt and freshly ground pepper

1 small clove garlic, chopped

Leaves from 1 bunch fresh flat-leaf parsley, finely chopped

6–8 leaves fresh mint, cut into slivers

1 lb (500 g) fresh English peas, shelled

½ cup (4 oz/125 g) crème fraîche

1 tsp Dijon mustard

Have ready a bowl of water to which you have added the lemon juice. Working with 1 artichoke at a time, pull off and discard the tough outer leaves until you reach the tender, pale yellow-green inner leaves. Cut off about 1 inch (2.5 cm) from the top to remove the prickly tips. Using a paring knife, remove the tough outer layer on the stem. Cut the trimmed artichokes lengthwise into quarters. As each artichoke is finished, drop it into the lemon water.

Warm a large sauté pan over medium-high heat and add the oil. Add the shallots and thyme sprig and sauté until fragrant, about 1 minute. Drain the artichokes, shake off the excess water, and add to the pan. Raise the heat to high, and cook, stirring occasionally, until the artichokes are lightly browned in places, about 5 minutes. Add the wine and cook until reduced to about 2 Tbsp, about 3 minutes. Add the broth and ½ tsp salt and bring to a boil. Reduce the heat to medium-low, cover, and simmer until the artichokes are tender when pierced with the tip of a paring knife, 12–15 minutes.

In a small bowl, mix together the garlic, parsley, mint, and lemon zest.

When the artichokes are done, there should be at least ½ cup (4 fl oz/125 ml) of liquid left in the pan. Add a little more broth if ⟫→

Thick, soft polenta (page 89) makes an ideal base for artichokes and peas, adding its own subtly sweet corn flavor. If you like, use a vegetable peeler to create Parmesan shavings as a garnish. You can substitute 1 cup (5 oz/155 g) frozen petite peas for the fresh ones if you can't find them.

needed. Add the peas, then stir in the crème fraîche and mustard. Cook, stirring, until the peas are warmed through, about 2 minutes.

Gently stir in the herb mixture, taste and adjust the seasonings, and serve.

2

PIZZA WITH GARLICKY SHRIMP, CHERRY TOMATOES & PARSLEY

serves 2–4

½ lb (250 g) small shrimp, peeled, deveined, and halved lengthwise

2 large cloves garlic, minced

½ tsp dried oregano

1 Tbsp olive oil, plus more as needed

All-purpose flour and cornmeal for dusting

1 lb (500 g) purchased whole-wheat pizza dough

Salt and freshly ground pepper

1 cup (6 oz/185 g) cherry tomatoes, halved

½ cup (½ oz/15 g) chopped fresh flat-leaf parsley

Position a rack in the bottom of the oven. Place a baking stone on the rack. Preheat the oven to 550°F (290°C), or the highest setting, for at least 45 minutes.

Meanwhile, in a bowl, toss the shrimp, garlic, oregano, and the 1 Tbsp oil to coat.

To assemble the pizza, lightly flour a work surface. Roll out the dough into a round 13–14 inches (33–35 cm) in diameter. Generously dust a pizza peel or rimless baking sheet with cornmeal and transfer the dough round to it. Working quickly, brush the raised edge of the dough with a light coating of oil and season generously with salt and pepper. Scatter the shrimp mixture and cherry tomatoes evenly over the dough, leaving a ½-inch (12-mm) border.

Immediately slide the pizza from the peel onto the baking stone. Bake until the crust is crisp and browned and the shrimp are pink, 10–12 minutes. Remove from the oven. Garnish the pizza with the chopped parsley, and serve.

Small shrimp rest like ruby gems atop this rustic pizza. Shrimp are full of selenium, an antioxidant that boosts immunity, making them a smart choice to top a pizza.

3

CARAMELIZED BEEF WITH ONIONS & WATERCRESS

serves 4–6

Filet mignon, one of the leanest cuts of beef, is cubed, steeped in a garlicy marinade, seared until a golden crust forms, then finished with a pat of butter for richness. Peppery watercress is high in vitamin A, calcium, and cancer-fighting substances and makes a perfect base for the tender meat.

6 cloves garlic, minced

½ small white onion, finely chopped

1 Tbsp Asian fish sauce

1 tsp sugar

Salt and freshly ground pepper

4 Tbsp (2 fl oz/60 ml) canola oil

1½ lb (750 g) filet mignon, cut into 1-inch (2.5-cm) cubes

1 small red onion, very thinly sliced

2 Tbsp rice vinegar

About 6 oz (185 g) watercress, tough stems removed

4 green onions, finely chopped

1 Tbsp unsalted butter

In a resealable plastic bag, combine the garlic, white onion, fish sauce, sugar, ¾ tsp salt, a generous grinding of pepper, and 2 Tbsp of the oil. Add the beef, squeeze out some of the air, seal the bag, and turn to distribute the ingredients. Let stand at room temperature or in the refrigerator for 1½–2 hours. If the beef is refrigerated, return it to room temperature before cooking.

In a small bowl, toss the red onion with the vinegar and plenty of pepper. Let stand for 10–15 minutes. Add 1 Tbsp of the oil and toss. Divide the watercress and green onions among plates and arrange some of the red onion on top.

Remove the beef from the bag and discard the marinade. Place a wok over high heat, add the remaining 1 Tbsp oil, and swirl to coat the pan. When the oil has just begun to shimmer, add the beef, distributing it evenly, and cook without moving it until golden brown, about 2 minutes. Turn, add the butter, and cook for about 1 minute more. Do not overcook the beef.

Arrange the beef and pan juices alongside the watercress, and serve.

4

FIVE-SPICE VEGETABLE & TOFU STIR-FRY

serves 4

Five-spice powder is typically a mix of ground fennel seeds, cinnamon, Sichuan pepper, cloves, and star anise. This highly aromatic medley works wonders on flavoring vegetables and tofu. Serve this dish with rice noodles or hot brown rice.

¾ lb (375 g) firm tofu, drained and cut into 1-inch (2.5-cm) cubes

Cornstarch for dusting

3 Tbsp canola oil

2–4 cloves garlic, chopped

1 Tbsp peeled and chopped fresh ginger

1 carrot, sliced on the diagonal

1 red bell pepper, seeded and diced

1 yellow onion, sliced lengthwise

1 head white cabbage, about 1½ lb (750 g), cut into large squares

Salt

½ tsp Chinese five-spice powder

4 Tbsp (2 fl oz/60 ml) low-sodium chicken broth

1 Tbsp sugar

3 Tbsp hoisin sauce

Low-sodium soy sauce, chile oil, and rice vinegar as needed

½ tsp Asian sesame oil

Blot the tofu dry, dust with the cornstarch, and blot again. In a wok, warm 1 Tbsp of the oil over medium-high heat. Add the tofu and cook until lightly browned on the first side, 3–4 minutes. Turn the tofu and continue cooking until browned on the opposite side, 3–4 minutes longer. Transfer to a plate. Wipe the pan clean, return it to high heat, and swirl in 1 Tbsp of the oil. Add the garlic, ginger, carrot, and bell pepper and stir-fry for 1 minute. Add to the plate with the tofu.

Return the pan to high heat and swirl in the remaining 1 Tbsp oil. Add the onion and stir-fry for 1 minute. Add the cabbage and a pinch of salt and stir-fry briefly. Mix in the five-spice powder and 3 Tbsp of the broth and stir-fry until the cabbage softens, 5–6 minutes. Stir in the sugar, hoisin, and a dash or two of the soy sauce and chile oil. Add another 1 Tbsp broth if the mixture seems dry. Cover and cook until the cabbage is almost tender-crisp, about 5 minutes. Uncover and add the carrot mixture and tofu. Stir-fry until heated through. Season with the vinegar. Transfer the vegetables to a platter, sprinkle with the sesame oil, and serve.

5

GRILLED SALMON WITH ASPARAGUS SLAW

serves 4

Shredded asparagus makes a wonderfully crunchy slaw that holds its texture well even when dressed and refrigerated. Using a cheese grater makes easy work of prepping the asparagus. Serve this dish atop a bed of arugula or fresh spinach.

1½ lb (750 g) skinless salmon fillets, cut on the diagonal into slices ½ inch (12 mm) thick

4 Tbsp (⅓ oz/10 g) finely chopped fresh cilantro

4 tsp olive oil

3 tsp low-sodium soy sauce

Grated zest and juice of 1 lime

1 Tbsp grapeseed oil

2 tsp Asian sesame oil

1 tsp grated fresh ginger

½ tsp sugar

Salt and freshly ground pepper

1 lb (500 g) asparagus, trimmed

2 oranges, peeled, segmented, and diced

2 green onions, thinly sliced

2 Tbsp toasted sesame seeds

Put the salmon in a bowl and add 2 Tbsp of the cilantro, the olive oil, 2 tsp of the soy sauce, and the lime zest. Turn the fish to coat evenly. Cover and refrigerate for 30 minutes.

To make the slaw, in a bowl, combine the lime juice, grapeseed and sesame oils, remaining 1 tsp soy sauce, the ginger, sugar, ½ tsp salt, and several grinds of pepper. Whisk thoroughly. Using the large holes on a box grater-shredder, shred the asparagus, discarding any woody or tough pieces. Place the asparagus shreds in a bowl. Add the oranges, green onions, remaining 2 Tbsp cilantro, and the sesame seeds. Pour over the lime-juice mixture and toss to mix well. Cover and refrigerate until ready to serve.

Prepare a grill for direct-heat cooking over medium heat. Arrange the salmon in a single layer in an oiled grilling basket. Sprinkle the fillets with a little pepper. Place the basket on the grill, cover the grill, and cook, turning once, until the fish is still slightly translucent in the center, about 3 minutes per side. Transfer the fish to a platter, tent with foil, and let rest for 3–4 minutes.

Divide the salmon among warmed plates, top with the slaw, and serve.

6

BLACK BEAN TACOS WITH AVOCADO SALSA

serves 4

Rich in fiber and a source of plant-based protein, black beans are a perfect stand-in for meat or chicken in these easy vegetarian tacos. Serve with a green salad tossed with jicama and oranges.

1 white onion, finely chopped

2 large plum tomatoes, halved, seeded, and finely diced

¼ cup (⅓ oz/10 g) minced fresh cilantro

3 Tbsp fresh lime juice, plus lime wedges for garnish

1 serrano chile, seeded and minced

1 avocado, pitted, peeled, and finely diced

Salt and freshly ground pepper

2 Tbsp olive oil

1 large red bell pepper, diced

½ cup (3 oz/185 g) thawed frozen corn kernels

12 small corn tortillas

¼ tsp fennel seeds

2 cans (15 oz/470 g each) black beans, drained, liquid reserved

Feta cheese, crumbled

In a bowl, stir together ¼ cup (1 oz/30 g) onion with the tomatoes, cilantro, lime juice, and chile. Gently mix in the avocado. Season the mixture with salt and pepper.

In a large frying pan over medium-high heat, warm 1 Tbsp of the oil. Add the bell pepper, season with salt and pepper, and sauté until it starts to soften, about 7 minutes. Add the corn kernels, reduce the heat to medium, and sauté until they begin to soften, about 2 minutes. Adjust the seasoning with salt and pepper. Transfer the mixture to a bowl and cover to keep warm.

Toast the tortillas over a gas flame or on a griddle just until warmed, about 20 seconds on each side. Wrap the tortillas in foil to keep warm. In the same frying pan over medium heat, warm the remaining 1 Tbsp oil. Add the remaining onion and the fennel seeds, and sauté until almost tender, about 5 minutes. Add the beans, and mash and stir the mixture until a coarse, thick purée forms, adding the reserved bean liquid as needed. Season with salt and pepper.

Place the salsa, bell pepper mixture, bean mixture, cheese, tortillas, and lime wedges on the table and serve, allowing diners to assemble their own tacos.

7

SQUID SALAD WITH ORANGES, FAVA BEANS & FENNEL

serves 4–6

1½ lb (750 g) fava beans, shelled

Salt and freshly ground pepper

1½ lb (750 g) cleaned squid, bodies cut into ½-inch (12-mm) rings and tentacles coarsely chopped

2 oranges

2 stalks celery, chopped

1 small fennel bulb, halved and thinly sliced

3 Tbsp chopped fresh flat-leaf parsley

Grated zest and juice of 1 lemon

1 Tbsp red wine vinegar

1 tsp Dijon mustard

3 Tbsp extra-virgin olive oil

This make-ahead salad is loaded with fresh flavors and different textures. Fennel is rich in vitamins and nutrients that benefit nearly every part of the body. The slight licorice taste and crunch of the fennel is balanced by sweet, juicy oranges. Flash-boiled fava beans and squid are added for a double dose of low-fat protein.

Bring a saucepan three-fourths full of water to a boil and add the favas. Boil for 1 minute, then use a skimmer to transfer them to a bowl. Squeeze each bean free of its tough outer skin. Put the beans in a bowl.

Bring the water back to a boil. Add 1 tsp salt and the squid and cook until the squid is opaque and just cooked through, about 90 seconds. Drain and immediately plunge into a bowl filled with ice water. Drain again and pat dry with paper towels. Transfer the squid to the bowl with the fava beans.

Grate the zest from 1 orange into a bowl. Cut a slice off both ends of each orange so they will stand upright. Stand them on a cutting board and, using a large, sharp knife, cut away the peel and white pith by slicing from top to bottom, following the contour of the fruit. Using a small knife, and working over the bowl with the zest to capture the juices, cut along either side of each segment to free it from the membrane and let it fall into the bowl. Add the orange segments, zest, and juices to the bowl with the squid. Add the celery, fennel, parsley, and lemon zest and stir to combine.

In a small bowl, combine the lemon juice, red wine vinegar, and Dijon mustard. Slowly whisk in the olive oil. Season with salt and pepper. Pour the mixture over the squid and toss to combine. Season again with salt and pepper, cover, and refrigerate for at least 1 hour before serving.

8

VIETNAMESE-STYLE RICE NOODLES WITH TOFU & MINT

serves 6

½ lb (250 g) banh hoi (Vietnamese rice vermicelli), broken into 2-inch (5-cm) pieces

½ lb (250 g) firm tofu, drained well

2 Tbsp cornstarch

6 Tbsp (3 fl oz/90 ml) grapeseed oil

Salt

⅓ cup (3 fl oz/80 ml) Asian fish sauce

¼ cup (2 oz/60 g) sweet chile sauce

1 Tbsp brown sugar

1 Tbsp fresh lime juice

1 tsp Sriracha sauce

¼ cup (¼ oz/7 g) bean sprouts

¼ cup (¾ oz/20 g) thinly sliced green onions

½ cup (½ oz/15 g) fresh mint leaves, thinly sliced

½ cup (½ oz/15 g) fresh basil leaves, thinly sliced

This easy dish is surprisingly healthful. Mint is a naturally soothing herb that also has anti-bacterial qualities. Basil adds sweet and spicy flavor, and anti-inflammatory compounds. Serve this soup with extra Sriracha and soy sauce at the table.

Place the banh hoi in a heatproof bowl and cover with very hot tap water. Let the noodles soak until tender and opaque, about 10 minutes. Drain well.

Place the tofu in a shallow dish and cover with a plate. Place a heavy can or weight on the plate and let stand for at least 15 minutes or up to 1 hour to remove excess moisture. Cut the tofu into ½-inch (6-mm) cubes and toss the cubes in the cornstarch to coat.

Heat the oil over medium-high heat in a large sauté pan. When the oil is hot, carefully add the tofu. Cook until well browned on all sides, 3–4 minutes per side. Transfer the tofu to a paper towel–lined plate to drain and sprinkle with a pinch of salt.

In a large bowl, combine the fish sauce, chile sauce, brown sugar, lime juice, and Sriracha. Add the bean sprouts, green onions, tofu, and noodles and toss to mix well. Garnish with the mint and basil, and serve warm or at room temperature.

9

FLANK STEAK STUFFED WITH ASPARAGUS PESTO

serves 4–6

*Pesto can be made
from virtually
any green, leafy
vegetable or herb,
and even some
stalks, like
asparagus. Here,
par-boiled asparagus
blends beautifully
into a pesto with
bright green color
and earthy flavor.
The fiber-rich
paste is spiraled
into a juicy roll
of flank steak for a
festive presentation.
Any leftover pesto
is delicious on
pasta, spread
on whole-grain
bruschetta with
fresh mozzarella,
or as a filling
for an omelet.*

FOR THE ASPARAGUS PESTO

½ tsp salt

¾ lb (375 g) asparagus, trimmed

3 Tbsp pine nuts

2 cloves garlic

Grated zest of 1 lemon

½ cup (2 oz/60 g) grated Parmesan cheese

6 Tbsp (3 fl oz/90 ml) olive oil

FOR THE FLANK STEAK

1–1¾ lb (500–875 g) flank steak, butterflied

Salt and freshly ground pepper

2 tsp olive oil

To make the pesto, bring a saucepan of water to a boil over high heat. Add the salt and asparagus and cook just until tender, about 4 minutes. Drain and immediately plunge into a bowl filled with ice water to stop the cooking. Drain well. Transfer the asparagus, pine nuts, and garlic to a food processor and pulse to finely chop. Add the lemon zest, Parmesan, and oil and purée until smooth. Season with salt and set aside.

Preheat the oven to 400°F (200°C). Lay the steak flat on a work surface and season with salt and pepper. Spread a ¼-inch (6-mm) layer of the pesto over the top of the steak, leaving about a ½-inch (12-mm) border around the edges. Roll the steak up with the grain and lay it seam-side down on the work surface. Using kitchen twine, tie the steak roll in 4 different spots, each about 2 inches (5 cm) apart.

In a large frying pan over high heat, warm the 2 tsp oil. Add the flank steak and sear until browned, about 3 minutes per side. Transfer the steak to a baking sheet and place in the oven. Roast until the center of the meat registers about 125°F (52°C) on a meat thermometer, 20–25 minutes. Let the steak rest for 10 minutes.

Remove the strings, slice the steak, and serve.

10

HERBED VEGETABLE STEW

serves 6

*Turnips, fava beans,
and potatoes make
this all-vegetable
stew extra-hearty.
Baby carrots, tiny
peas, and tender
leeks add morsels
of flavor and
nutrients. Serve this
stew over whole-
wheat couscous
mixed with sliced
toasted almonds.*

12 baby turnips, trimmed

1½ lb (750 g) fava beans, shelled

1½ lb (750 g) English peas, shelled

5 Tbsp (3 fl oz/80 g) olive oil

1½ cups (2½ oz/75 g) chopped shallots

1 cup (8 fl oz/250 ml) dry white wine

3 cups (24 fl oz/750 ml) low-sodium vegetable or chicken broth

18 small red potatoes

Salt and freshly ground pepper

18 baby carrots

1½ cups (1½ oz/45 g) chopped tender leek greens, plus 8 small leeks, white part only, cut into 2-inch (5-cm) lengths

¼ cup (⅓ oz/10 g) finely snipped fresh chives

2 Tbsp *each* minced fresh tarragon and flat-leaf parsley

Place the turnips on a steamer rack over boiling water, cover, and steam until tender, 8–10 minutes. Set aside.

Bring a saucepan three-fourths full of water to a boil and add the fava beans. Boil for 1 minute, then use a skimmer to transfer them to a bowl. Squeeze each bean free of its tough outer skin. Place the favas and peas on the steamer rack over boiling water, cover, and steam until tender, 6–7 minutes.

In a large, heavy saucepan over medium-high heat, warm 4 Tbsp (2 fl oz/60 ml) of the oil. Add the shallots and sauté until translucent, 6–7 minutes. Pour in the wine and stir to scrape up the browned bits from the pan bottom. Add the broth, potatoes, 1 tsp salt, and 2 tsp pepper. Cover tightly, reduce the heat to medium-low, and simmer for 10 minutes.

Uncover the saucepan and stir in the carrots and leek greens; arrange the white parts of the leeks on top. Cover and cook until the carrots and potatoes are almost tender, 8–10 minutes longer. Uncover and add the turnips, peas, and favas, turning them gently in the simmering stew. Re-cover and cook until all the vegetables are tender, 6–7 minutes longer. Season with salt. Stir in all but about 1 tsp each of the chives, tarragon, and parsley.

Serve, garnished with the remaining herbs.

11

MAY

This is a great dish for entertaining or a family dinner, as the food is cooked right at the table. To make the sesame-soy dipping sauce, whisk together 3 Tbsp low-sodium soy sauce, 2 Tbsp dark soy sauce, 2 Tbsp rice vinegar, 1 Tbsp Asian sesame oil, 1 tsp each chile oil and Sriracha sauce, 2 minced green onions, 2 minced garlic cloves, and 2 tsp sugar until the sugar dissolves. Stir in 3 Tbsp warm water.

MONGOLIAN HOT POT

serves 4–6

½ lb (250 g) *each* beef sirloin, pork tenderloin, and peeled medium shrimp

6 Tbsp (3 fl oz/90ml) low-sodium soy sauce

3 Tbsp Chinese rice wine

1 Tbsp Asian sesame oil

2 tsp sugar

Salt and freshly ground pepper

8 cups (64 fl oz/2 l) low-sodium chicken broth

Soy-Sesame Dipping Sauce (see Note)

½ head napa cabbage, cored

¼ lb (125 g) shiitake mushrooms, stems removed

3 oz (90 g) cellophane noodles, soaked in boiling water for 15 minutes and drained

14 oz (440 g) firm tofu, cut into 1-inch (2.5-cm) cubes

1 bunch watercress

Cut the beef and pork across the grain into slices ⅛ inch (4 mm) thick. Place the beef, pork, and shrimp in 3 separate bowls. In another bowl, whisk together 3 Tbsp of the soy sauce, 2 Tbsp of the rice wine, the sesame oil, 1 tsp of the sugar, and ⅛ tsp pepper. Pour one-third of the soy sauce mixture into each bowl holding the meat or shrimp. Stir well. Marinate at room temperature for 1 hour.

In a large saucepan, combine the broth, remaining 3 Tbsp soy sauce, 1 Tbsp rice wine, 1 tsp sugar, 1 tsp salt, and ⅛ tsp pepper and bring to a boil over high heat. Reduce the heat to low and simmer the soup for 10 minutes to blend the flavors.

Set up a portable electric burner on the dining table, pour the soup into a pot, and place on the burner. Divide the dipping sauce among small bowls and set on the table. Cut the cabbage leaves into 2-inch (5-cm) squares. Cut the mushrooms into slices ¼ inch (6 mm) thick. On a platter, arrange the cabbage, mushrooms, noodles, tofu, and watercress. Place the marinated beef, pork, and shrimp in separate serving bowls.

When ready to eat, instruct diners to add the vegetables, noodles, and tofu to the soup and simmer for about 5 minutes. Next, ask them to add meat and shrimp of their choice and cook to the desired doneness (about 1 minute for the meat and 2 minutes for the shrimp) ⟫⟫

and then place in their bowls. Using a slotted spoon, divide the vegetables, tofu, and noodles among the individual bowls. Guests can dip them in the dipping sauce or drizzle the sauce on top. When all the vegetables, meat, and shrimp are eaten, ladle the hot soup into the individual bowls to finish the meal.

12

MAY

This recipe is a healthy spin on German-style schnitzel. Whole-wheat bread crumbs add a hearty crunch to the lean pork cutlets. Arugula lends peppery flavor, vitamin C, and calcium as well as anticancer phytochemicals to the meal.

PORK SCHNITZEL & ARUGULA

serves 4

2 lemons

1½ cups (3 oz/90 g) coarse fresh whole-wheat bread crumbs

⅓ cup (1½ oz/45 g) all-purpose flour

Salt and freshly ground pepper

1 egg

4 pork cutlets, about 1½ lb (750 g) total, pounded until about ½-inch (12-mm) thick

4 Tbsp (2 fl oz/60 ml) olive oil

1 shallot, minced

6 cups (6 oz/185 g) arugula, tough stems removed

Finely grate 2 tsp zest and squeeze 2 Tbsp juice from 1 lemon. Cut the second lemon into 8 wedges. Spread the bread crumbs on a plate. In a shallow bowl, stir together the flour, lemon zest, ½ tsp salt, and ¼ tsp pepper. In another shallow bowl, beat the egg with 1 Tbsp water. Working with 1 cutlet at a time, dredge it in the flour mixture, shaking off the excess. Next, dip the cutlet in the egg, letting the excess drip back into the bowl. Finally, dip the cutlet in the bread crumbs, patting firmly to adhere.

In a large frying pan over medium-high heat, warm 2 Tbsp of the oil. Add the cutlets and cook, turning once, until golden-brown and cooked through, 4–6 minutes total. Transfer to a plate. Add the remaining 2 Tbsp oil to the pan over medium heat. Add the shallot and sauté until softened, about 1 minute. Stir in the lemon juice, scraping up the browned bits on the pan bottom. Remove from the heat, add the arugula, and toss briefly to coat. Divide the cutlets among 4 plates, top with the arugula, garnish with the lemon wedges, and serve.

13

POLENTA GRIDDLE CAKES WITH CHICKEN & CHERRY SALSA

serves 4

¾ lb (375 g) boneless, skinless chicken thighs

2 tsp olive oil

Salt and freshly ground pepper

FOR THE POLENTA GRIDDLE CAKES

1 cup (5 oz/155 g) polenta

1 Tbsp butter, melted

½ tsp salt, plus more for seasoning

3¼ cups (28 fl oz/875 ml) warm water

2 tsp olive oil

FOR THE CHERRY SALSA

½ lb (250 g) fresh cherries, pitted and chopped

Juice of ½ lime

1 small jalapeño chile, minced

2 Tbsp minced fresh cilantro

¼ cup (1¼ oz/37 g) crumbled cotija cheese

Cherries often evoke sweet desserts, but here's a great idea for a savory dish. The fruit adds deep color and tartness (the darker the cherry, the richer it is in anti-oxidants) while skinless chicken provides lean protein. Look for stone-ground, yellow corn polenta to ensure you're getting a whole-grain, full of golden carotenoids, which protect your eyes and heart.

Preheat the oven to 400°F (200°C). Brush the chicken with oil and season with salt and pepper. Roast until opaque throughout, about 25 minutes. Cook, then shred and set aside. Reduce the oven heat to 350°F (180°C).

To make the polenta cakes, mix together the polenta, melted butter, ½ tsp salt, and warm water in a bowl. Pour into a 9-by-13-inch (23-by-33-cm) glass baking dish, taking care that all of the solid ingredients are evenly distributed in the bottom of the pan. Place on the middle oven rack and bake until firm, about 55 minutes. Cool to room temperature.

Meanwhile, to make the salsa, combine the cherries, lime juice, jalapeño, and cilantro in a bowl and stir to combine. Let stand, stirring occasionally, until ready to serve.

Using a 3-inch (7.5-cm) round cutter, carefully cut out 8 circles from the pan of polenta, using a flat spatula to lift them from the pan. Brush each side of the polenta cakes lightly with the 2 tsp oil and season with salt. Warm a frying pan over high heat. When hot, add the polenta cakes and sauté until golden brown, about 3 minutes per side.

Arrange 2 polenta cakes on each plate. Top with the shredded chicken, cherry salsa, and cheese, dividing evenly, and serve.

14

BUCKWHEAT NOODLE SALAD WITH SHRIMP

serves 6

Salt

1 lb (500 g) buckwheat soba noodles

¼ cup (2 fl oz/60 ml) rice wine vinegar

3 Tbsp soy sauce

1 tsp Asian chile oil

1 Tbsp grapeseed oil

1 Tbsp wasabi paste, or to taste

1 lb (500 g) medium shrimp, peeled and deveined

2 cups (2 oz/60 g) watercress

1 English cucumber, halved, seeded and cut into ¼-inch (6-mm) half-moons

1 red jalapeño chile, seeded and finely diced

Buckwheat has been shown to contribute to cardiovascular health. It's also gluten-free, so it's a good substitute for wheat noodles if you have a gluten sensitivity. Here, thin buckwheat noodles are served chilled in a spicy Asian sauce, with familiar flavors, such as soy sauce and wasabi paste. Paired with lean shrimp and piquant watercress, it's a perfect dish for a warm day.

Bring a large pot of generously salted water to a boil over high heat. Add the soba noodles and cook until al dente, 4–6 minutes. Drain the noodles and rinse under cold running water until cool. Put in a large bowl.

In a small bowl, whisk together the vinegar, soy sauce, chile oil, grapeseed oil, and wasabi paste to make a sauce. Reserve 2 Tbsp of the sauce and place the rest in a small serving bowl.

Toss the shrimp with the reserved 2 Tbsp sauce. Warm a sauté pan over medium heat. When the pan is hot, add the shrimp and sauté just until pink, 2–4 minutes. Remove the shrimp from the pan and set aside.

To serve, toss the noodles with the watercress and half of the reserved sauce. Arrange the mixture on a platter and top with the shrimp, cucumber, and jalapeño. Drizzle the remaining sauce over the top, and serve.

15

Stir-fries are perfect for weeknights because they require minimal preparation, cook in minutes, and can be composed of whatever protein and vegetables you have on hand. Serve with brown rice or toss some leftover cooked brown rice directly into the wok for the last 2 minutes of cooking.

CHICKEN & ASPARAGUS STIR-FRY

serves 4

2 Tbsp peanut oil

1½ lb (750 g) boneless, skinless chicken breast halves, cut into thin strips

2 Tbsp minced fresh ginger

1 stalk lemongrass, bulb part only, finely chopped

3 cloves garlic, minced

½ lb (250 g) asparagus, cut on the diagonal into 1-inch (2.5-cm) lengths

¾ cup (6 fl oz/180 ml) low-sodium chicken broth

2 Tbsp Asian fish sauce

¼ cup (1½ oz/45 g) chopped roasted peanuts

Heat a wok over high heat until very hot, about 2 minutes. Swirl in the oil. Add the chicken, spread out in a single layer, and cook, undisturbed, for 20–30 seconds. Stir-fry the chicken until opaque throughout, about 1 minute more. Transfer to a plate.

Add the ginger, lemongrass, and garlic to the pan and stir-fry until fragrant, about 30 seconds. Add the asparagus and stir-fry until tender-crisp, 2–3 minutes.

Add the broth and fish sauce to the pan and bring to a simmer. Return the chicken and any juices from the plate to the pan, reduce the heat to medium-low, and simmer until heated through, about 1 minute.

Divide the stir-fry among warmed plates, top with the peanuts, and serve.

16

Fresh, light, and satisfying are the first words that come to mind for this inspired salad. This salad has a base of farro for nutty texture and good carbohydrates. Store cooked farro, hard-boiled eggs, and chopped vegetables separately for making extra salads later in the week.

FARRO SALAD

serves 4

1 cup (5 oz/155 g) farro

Salt and freshly ground pepper

4–6 radishes, trimmed and thinly sliced

2 tomatoes, chopped

1 Persian cucumber, chopped

⅓ cup (2 oz/60 g) chopped pitted black olives

¼ cup (¼ oz/7 g) fresh basil leaves, cut into thin slivers

3 Tbsp extra-virgin olive oil

Lettuce leaves (optional)

4 hard-boiled eggs, peeled and quartered

Put the farro in a large pot along with 4 cups (32 fl oz/1 l) water. Bring to a boil and add 1 tsp salt. Reduce the heat to low and simmer until just tender, about 25–30 minutes.

Drain the farro and pour it into a large bowl. Add the radishes, tomatoes, cucumber, olives, basil, and oil and toss well. Season with salt and pepper.

Line plates with lettuce leaves, if using, and spoon the farro mixture over the top. Divide the egg quarters among the plates, and serve.

17

LAMB & ARTICHOKE SPIEDINI

serves 4–6

1¼ lb (625 g) boneless lamb leg steaks, trimmed and cut into ¾ inch (2-cm) cubes

1 lb (500 g) thawed frozen artichoke hearts

Grated zest and juice of 1 lemon, plus lemon wedges for serving

3 Tbsp olive oil, plus more for brushing

2 cloves garlic, minced

2 tsp minced fresh oregano

Salt and freshly ground pepper

Spiedini is the Italian version of kebabs—meat is cubed and marinated in a simple mixture of herbs and skewered with Italian-style vegetables. Roasted red peppers would make a great addition. Serve the spiedini over polenta (page 89) for fiber and whole-grain goodness.

In a bowl, combine the lamb, artichokes, lemon zest and juice, 3 Tbsp oil, garlic, and oregano. Add ½ tsp salt and season with pepper. Toss to combine and let stand at room temperature for 1 hour, or cover and refrigerate for at least 2 hours or up to 6 hours. Toss the mixture occasionally. Soak 14 wooden skewers in water for 30 minutes.

Prepare a grill or stove-top grill pan for direct-heat cooking over medium-high heat. Thread the ingredients onto each skewer, dividing them evenly. Position them close to the pointed end of the skewer, and press the lamb pieces snugly together. Oil the grill rack.

Place the skewers on the grill rack over the hottest part of the fire or in the grill pan, and cook until browned, about 2½ minutes. Turn and cook until browned and just firm to the touch, 2–3 minutes more. Arrange the skewers on a warmed platter. Season with salt and garnish with lemon wedges.

18

CHILE-LIME TOFU WITH BOK CHOY

serves 4

3 Tbsp low-sodium soy sauce

2 Tbsp honey

2 Tbsp fresh lime juice

1 Tbsp canola oil, plus 2 tsp

A few drops of Asian sesame oil

2 cloves garlic, minced

½ tsp red chile flakes

1 package (14 oz/440 g) extra-firm tofu, cut in half lengthwise and then cut into ½-inch (12-mm) slices

Nonstick cooking spray

4 heads baby bok choy, quartered lengthwise

This heart-healthy dish is rich in isoflavones thanks to the plant-based proteins in tofu. Don't skimp on bok choy—it's virtually calorie free, loaded in vitamin C, and has a high water density. Serve this dish with brown rice or buckwheat noodles for a light Asian-style meal. Any leftover marinade is delicious on fish or chicken.

In a small bowl, combine the soy sauce, honey, lime juice, 1 Tbsp canola oil, the sesame oil, garlic, and chile flakes. Stir until the honey dissolves. Place the tofu in a dish and pour in the marinade, taking care that all the tofu is covered by the marinade. Cover and refrigerate for at least 1 hour, turning the tofu once.

Warm a large nonstick frying pan over medium-high heat and coat lightly with cooking spray. Remove the tofu from the marinade, reserving the marinade, and add it to the pan. Sauté until the tofu is golden brown, about 3 minutes per side. Transfer to a plate.

In the same frying pan, warm the 2 tsp canola oil until it is very hot, but not smoking. Add the bok choy and cook, using tongs to turn, until it is golden brown, 3–4 minutes. Pour 3 Tbsp of the reserved marinade around the pan, and toss and stir just until most of the liquid is absorbed and the bok choy is lightly glazed.

Put the tofu back into the pan and warm for a minute or two. Divide the tofu and bok choy among 4 plates, and serve.

19

Wheat berries are whole-wheat kernels, similar to brown rice in appearance, with a nutty, earthy flavor and chewy bite. Because wheat berries are unprocessed, they retain all the whole grain benefits, such as fiber, after cooking. Together, the artichokes, pork, and wheat berries make a balanced meal of vegetables, protein, and whole grain. Serve this with a butter lettuce salad for additional vegetables.

SPICED PORK WITH ARTICHOKES & WHEAT BERRIES

serves 4

2 tsp ground cumin

1 tsp *each* dried oregano and ground coriander

½ tsp garlic powder

Salt and freshly ground pepper

½ lb (250 g) pork tenderloin

2 Tbsp olive oil plus 1 tsp

1 lemon, halved

4 artichokes, trimmed

2 cloves garlic, chopped

1 cup (6 oz/185 g) cherry tomatoes, halved

1 cup (6 oz/185 g) wheat berries, cooked according to package directions

¼ cup (⅓ oz/10 g) chopped fresh basil

Preheat the oven to 400°F (200°C). In a small bowl, combine the cumin, oregano, coriander, garlic powder, ½ tsp salt, and a few grinds of pepper. Rub the spice mixture all over the pork. In a frying pan over high heat, warm the 1 tsp oil. Add the pork and sear until browned on all sides, about 8 minutes total. Transfer the pork to a baking sheet and roast in the oven until it reaches an internal temperature of 140°F (60°C), about 25 minutes. Let rest for 10 minutes and then cut into 1-inch (2.5-cm) pieces.

Bring a large pot of water to a boil over high heat. Have ready a bowl of water with the juice of ½ lemon. Working with 1 artichoke at a time, pull off and discard the tough outer leaves until you reach the tender, pale yellow-green inner leaves. Cut off about 1 inch (2.5 cm) from the top to remove the prickly tips. Cut off the stem end even with the bottom. Cut the trimmed artichokes into eighths and cut out the fuzzy chokes. Add the artichokes to the bowl with the lemon water. Add 1 tsp of salt to the boiling water and add the drained artichokes. Cook until they are tender, about 12 minutes. Drain.

In a frying pan over medium-low heat, warm the remaining 2 Tbsp oil. Add the garlic and sauté until softened, about 2 minutes. Add the tomatoes and sauté just until they begin to release their juices but still hold their shape, about 2 minutes. Transfer the ⟫→

garlic and tomatoes to a large serving bowl and add the wheat berries, basil, pork, and artichokes. Stir to mix, season with salt and pepper, and stir in the juice of the remaining ½ lemon, and serve.

20

Use purchased whole-wheat pizza dough for an easy dish you can throw together at the last minute. You won't find any tomatoes on this non-traditional green-and-white pizza. The base is a creamy, low-fat mixture of basil and ricotta. It's topped with a medley of nearly caramelized leeks and asparagus. Pay special attention when cleaning the leeks—it's best to chop them, and let them soak in a bowl of cold water until the dirt embedded between the leaves falls to the bottom.

PIZZA WITH ASPARAGUS, LEEKS & HERBED RICOTTA

serves 4

Flour and cornmeal, for dusting

1 lb (500 g) purchased whole-wheat pizza dough, rolled out to ⅛-inch thickness

3 Tbsp olive oil, divided

Salt and freshly ground pepper

1 cup (8 oz/250 g) part-skim ricotta cheese

2 Tbsp chopped fresh basil

3 leeks, cleaned and chopped

3 cloves garlic, chopped

1 bunch thin asparagus, tough ends trimmed, cut into 3-inch (7.5-cm) pieces

Position a rack in the bottom of the oven. Place a baking stone on the rack. Preheat the oven to 550°F (290°C), or the highest setting, for at least 45 minutes.

To assemble the pizza, lightly flour a work surface. Roll out the dough into a round 13–14 inches (33–35 cm) in diameter. Generously dust a pizza peel or rimless baking sheet with cornmeal and transfer the dough round to it. Brush the top of the pizza with 1 Tbsp of the oil and season all over with salt and pepper. In a small bowl, stir together the cheese and basil. Season with salt and pepper. Spread the ricotta mixture over the dough in a thick, even layer.

In a frying pan over medium-high heat, warm the remaining 2 Tbsp oil. Add the leeks and garlic, season with salt and pepper, and sauté until soft, about 5 minutes. Add the asparagus, stir to coat with the oil, and cook just until the asparagus begins to soften, about 3 minutes. Spread the leeks and asparagus evenly over the ricotta mixture. Immediately slide the pizza from the peel onto the baking stone. Bake until the crust is crisp and browned, 10–12 minutes. Remove from the oven, let cool slightly, and serve.

21

This dish is comprised of ingredients you may already have on hand in your pantry. It's a great hearty, yet healthy dish to keep in mind for busy days.

WHOLE-WHEAT PENNE WITH WHITE BEANS & ARUGULA

serves 4–6

Salt and freshly ground pepper

¾ lb (375 g) dried whole-wheat penne

1 Tbsp olive oil

½ red onion, chopped

½ tsp red pepper flakes

3 large cloves garlic, chopped

1 can (15 oz/470 g) cannellini beans, undrained

2 oz (60 g) baby arugula

4 Tbsp (1 oz/30 g) grated pecorino romano cheese

Bring a large pot full of salted water to a boil. Add the penne, stir well, and cook until al dente, 10–12 minutes, or according to package directions.

Meanwhile, in a large nonstick frying pan over medium heat, warm the oil. Add the onion and pepper flakes and sauté until the onion is tender, about 5 minutes. Add the garlic and the beans with their liquid and sauté until the beans are heated through, about 2 minutes. Add the arugula and continue to stir until wilted and heated through, about 1 minute.

Drain the pasta, transfer it to the pan with the bean-arugula mixture, and toss well. Sprinkle with the cheese and season with salt and pepper. Divide among warmed plates, and serve.

22

Mood-boosting capsaicin, the active spicy component in poblano chiles stimulates feel-good endorphins, suppresses appetite, and raises metabolism. Radishes offer a peppery crunch, and omega 3–rich avocados offer healthy fat in place of cheese. Held together in a warm, chewy corn tortilla, these tacos are naturally gluten-free.

STEAK & CHILE TACOS WITH AVOCADO-RADISH SALSA

serves 4

1 poblano chile

1 lb (500 g) skirt steak

1 tsp canola oil

Salt and freshly ground pepper

FOR THE AVOCADO-RADISH SALSA

6 radishes, trimmed, halved, and thinly sliced

1 firm but ripe avocado, cubed

Juice of ½ lime

1 Tbsp chopped fresh cilantro

Salt and freshly ground pepper

Juice of ½ lime

8 small white corn tortillas, lightly grilled or warmed in the oven

Preheat the broiler. Cut the chile in half lengthwise and place it on a baking sheet. Broil, turning as needed, until the skin is completely charred and black, about 5 minutes. Transfer the chile to a bowl and cover with a clean kitchen towel. Let steam for 10 minutes, then remove the blackened skin. Seed the chile and cut it into thin strips.

Warm a stove-top grill pan over high heat. Brush the steak with the oil and season both sides with salt and pepper. When the pan is very hot, add the steak and cook until medium-rare in the center, about 3 minutes per side. Transfer the steak to a cutting board and let rest for 10 minutes.

To make the salsa, in a small bowl, gently toss the radishes, avocado, lime juice, and cilantro. Season with salt and pepper.

Slice the steak against the grain and drizzle with the lime juice.

To serve, fill each tortilla with steak, chile strips, and a spoonful of the salsa.

23

ROASTED SALMON WITH THYME VINAIGRETTE & BABY LETTUCES

serves 4

Sustainable wild Alaskan king salmon, rich in omega-3 fats, starts its season in early spring. A salad of mixed baby lettuces makes a vivid and light accompaniment. Smashed young potatoes would round out the meal perfectly.

1 Tbsp Dijon mustard

1 Tbsp white wine vinegar

¼ cup (2 fl oz/60 ml) extra-virgin olive oil

2 Tbsp minced shallot

1 Tbsp minced fresh thyme

Salt and freshly ground pepper

2 salmon fillets, about 1½ lb (750 g)

6 cups (6 oz/185 g) mixed baby lettuces

Preheat the oven to 425°F (220°C). In a small bowl, whisk together the mustard and vinegar. Gradually whisk in the ¼ cup (2 fl oz/60 ml) oil. Stir in the shallot and thyme. Season the vinaigrette to taste with salt and pepper. Brush a small baking dish with oil. Place the salmon in the dish, skin side down. Spoon half the vinaigrette over the salmon. Let marinate for 15–20 minutes at room temperature, or refrigerate for up to 1 hour.

Roast the salmon until almost cooked through, about 15 minutes. Let it rest while preparing the salad.

In a bowl, toss the lettuces with the remaining vinaigrette.

Divide the salad among plates. Cut each salmon fillet in half and put one piece alongside the salad on each plate.

24

SHRIMP SUMMER ROLLS

serves 2–4

Nuoc cham, a sweet and spicy Vietnamese dipping sauce, adds lively flavor to these fresh vegetable-and-shrimp rolls. Don't skimp on the herbs, as they offer beneficial phytochemicals. The rolls will keep at room temperature for several hours before serving if they are well covered with plastic wrap.

FOR THE NUOC CHAM

3 cloves garlic, chopped

1½ Tbsp sugar

3 Tbsp Asian fish sauce

2 Tbsp *each* rice vinegar and fresh lime juice

1 serrano chile, seeded and thinly sliced

1 Tbsp *each* grated carrot and daikon

2 oz (60 g) cellophane noodles, soaked in boiling water for 15 minutes

6 rice-paper rounds, each 8 inches (20 cm) in diameter

6 red-leaf lettuce leaves

1 small carrot, shredded

½ small cucumber, peeled, seeded, and shredded

½ cup (½ oz/15 g) mung bean sprouts

6 cooked medium shrimp, cut in half lengthwise

18 *each* fresh mint leaves and cilantro leaves

To make the nuoc cham, put the garlic and sugar in a mini food processor and process until a paste forms. Transfer to a bowl and whisk in the fish sauce, vinegar, lime juice, and ¼ cup (2 fl oz/60 ml) water. Pour through a fine-mesh sieve into a clean bowl and add the chile, carrot, and daikon.

To assemble the rolls, drain the noodles. Fill a wide, shallow bowl with warm water. Soak 1 rice-paper round in the liquid until softened, 5 or 6 seconds. Remove it from the bowl, gently shake off the excess water, and place it on a work surface. Place a lettuce leaf horizontally on the bottom half of the rice paper. In a line across the base of the lettuce, place 1 tsp of the carrot, 1 tsp of the cucumber, several strands of the noodles, and several bean sprouts. Be careful not to overstuff the rolls. Lift the bottom edge of the rice paper and carefully roll up halfway into a tight cylinder. Place 2 shrimp halves and several mint and cilantro leaves tightly along the inside seam of the roll. Fold in the sides of the rice paper and continue to roll the rice paper and filling into a cylinder. Moisten the edge of the roll to seal. Repeat with the remaining ingredients. Cut the rolls in half on the diagonal and serve with the nuoc cham.

25

Pozole is a hearty stew seasoned with deep Mexican spices, fire-roasted tomatoes, and jalapeños. Hominy has a corn-like taste and chewy texture that is very filling when combined with melt-in-your-mouth pork tenderloin.

POZOLE

serves 4

2 Tbsp canola oil

1 lb (500 g) pork tenderloin, cut into ½-inch (12-mm) dice

1 yellow onion, finely chopped

3 cloves garlic, minced

1½ Tbsp chili powder

½ tsp ground cumin

½ tsp dried oregano

3 cups (24 fl oz/750 ml) low-sodium chicken broth

1 can (14½ oz/455 g) diced fire-roasted tomatoes

1 can (15 oz/470 g) white hominy, rinsed and drained

1 jalapeño chile, seeded and diced

Salt and freshly ground pepper

Avocado slices, for garnish

Sliced green onions, for garnish

Lime wedges, for serving

In a soup pot over medium heat, warm the oil. Working in batches if necessary, add the pork and sauté until opaque on all sides but not browned, about 3 minutes per batch. Using a slotted spoon, transfer the meat to a bowl and set aside.

Add the onion to the pot and sauté until softened, 3–5 minutes. Add the garlic, chili powder, cumin, and oregano and cook, stirring to blend the spices evenly, for about 1 minute longer. Add the broth, tomatoes, hominy, jalapeño, and sautéed pork with any juices, and season to taste with salt and pepper. Bring to a boil over high heat.

Reduce the heat to low, cover, and simmer until the pork is cooked through, about 15 minutes. If desired, test a piece of pork to ensure that it is fully cooked before serving.

To serve, ladle the soup into warmed bowls and garnish with the avocado slices and green onions. Serve with the lime wedges.

26

This fresh take on carpaccio pairs barely seared lean beef with an array of fresh herbs and warm spices. Try it as the star of a warm-weather lunch accompanied by grilled whole-grain bread. To make balsamic syrup, pour 2 cups (16 fl oz/500 ml) balsamic vinegar into a pan and cook over high heat until it's reduced to about ½ cup (4 fl oz/ 125 ml), about 15 minutes. Let it cool in a liquid measuring cup before using.

SEARED BEEF TENDERLOIN WITH CILANTRO & MINT

serves 4

1½ lb (750 g) beef tenderloin, trimmed

1 tsp ground ginger

1 tsp garlic powder

1 tsp onion powder

1 tsp cumin seeds, crushed

1 tsp coriander seeds, crushed

2 Tbsp chopped fresh cilantro, plus ⅓ cup (⅓ oz/10 g) fresh cilantro leaves

Coarse salt and freshly ground pepper

1 Tbsp Dijon mustard

2 Tbsp olive oil

6 fresh mint leaves, finely slivered

2 green onions, thinly sliced on the diagonal

2 Tbsp extra-virgin olive oil

Balsamic syrup, for drizzling (see Note)

Remove the beef from the refrigerator about 30 minutes before you plan to cook.

In a small bowl, stir together the ginger, garlic powder, onion powder, cumin, coriander, 2 Tbsp chopped cilantro, and 1 tsp each of salt and pepper. Spread the mixture on a large flat plate. Brush the beef on all sides with the mustard. Roll the beef in the spice mixture, coating it evenly and pressing the mixture lightly with your fingers so that it adheres to the surface.

In a large nonstick frying pan over high heat, warm the olive oil. When the oil is hot, add the meat and sear, turning as needed, until browned evenly on all sides, about 5 minutes; the meat will be rare in the center. Transfer the meat to a cutting board and let it rest for about 10 minutes.

Using a very sharp knife, slice against the grain as thinly as possible. Divide the slices evenly among 4 plates, folding the pieces and overlapping them slightly to cover the center of each plate. Scatter the cilantro leaves, mint, and green onions over the beef slices. Finish each plate with a drizzle of extra-virgin olive oil and balsamic syrup, and serve.

ROAST CHICKEN & BREAD SALAD WITH HARICOTS VERTS & STRAWBERRIES

serves 6–8

Nothing says summertime like a big family-style meal full of seasonal produce. Plump strawberries stand out as bright gems in this salad. The compounds that form strawberries' red color are considered anti-carcinogenic, which are substances that help prevent cancer. Haricot verts, French for green beans, add a fresh crunch and dose of vitamins A and C.

1 chicken (3 lb/1.5 kg),
cut into 8 serving pieces

5 Tbsp (3 fl oz/80 ml) olive oil

Salt and freshly ground pepper

8 oz (250 g) haricots verts or thin green beans

½ loaf crusty Italian bread,
cut into 1-inch (2.5-cm) cubes

1 shallot, minced

2 Tbsp red wine vinegar

2 Tbsp dried currants

¼ tsp Dijon mustard

1 pint (8 oz/250 g) strawberries,
hulled and thinly sliced

Preheat the oven to 400°F (200°C). Brush the chicken pieces with 2 Tbsp oil and place them on a baking sheet. Season well with salt and pepper and roast until an instant-read thermometer inserted into the thickest part of the thigh, not touching bone, reads 170°F (77°C), about 1 hour. Remove from the oven and reduce the oven temperature to 350°F (180°C).

Meanwhile, bring a saucepan of water to a boil over high heat. Add ½ tsp salt and the haricots verts and blanch just until slightly tender, about 2 minutes. Transfer to a colander and run under cold water to stop the cooking. Drain and set aside.

Toss the bread with 1 Tbsp of the oil and season with salt and pepper. Arrange the bread in a single layer on a baking sheet and bake until golden-brown, stirring once or twice, about 12 minutes.

In a small bowl, stir together the shallot, red wine vinegar, currants, and mustard. Slowly whisk in the remaining 2 Tbsp oil and season with salt and pepper to make a vinaigrette.

Place the haricots verts, strawberries, and croutons in a large bowl and add the vinaigrette. Toss to coat well and arrange on a large platter. Nestle the chicken pieces into the bread salad and serve.

HALIBUT CEVICHE WITH AVOCADO

serves 4–6

Ceviche is a raw fish dish which gets "cooked" from the acidity of the citrus juice in the marinade. This is a refreshing and easy summer dish that can be mixed with any of your favorite raw vegetables and herbs. Be sure to use impeccably fresh fish, and ask your fishmonger to be sure it's sushi-grade.

1¼ lb (600 g) fresh halibut fillets,
or other white fish fillets

½ cup (4 fl oz/125 ml) fresh lime juice

2 firm but ripe tomatoes, peeled,
seeded, and cut into small dice

2–3 serrano chiles, seeded and minced

⅓ cup (⅓ oz/10 g) chopped fresh cilantro

Salt and freshly ground pepper

1 avocado

10 green olives, preferably manzanillos,
pitted and coarsely chopped

1 tsp dried Mexican oregano

2 Tbsp extra-virgin olive oil

Baked tortilla chips for serving

Cut the fish fillets into small pieces and put them into a large glass bowl. Pour the lime juice over the fish, making sure all the pieces are covered. Cover and refrigerate for 3–4 hours; take care not to over-marinate.

Drain the fish and pat dry on paper towels. Put the fish cubes back into the bowl and add the tomatoes, chiles, cilantro, and salt and pepper to taste. Stir to mix well and refrigerate for about 2 hours.

When ready to serve, pit, peel, and dice the avocado and stir it into the fish mixture, along with the olives and oregano. Arrange the ceviche on a serving platter or plates and drizzle with the olive oil. Serve with tortilla chips for scooping.

GRILLED POLENTA WITH ROASTED VEGETABLES

serves 4

MAY

When shopping for polenta, look for a stone-ground, yellow corn variety, which offers all the benefits of a whole grain and is full of golden carotenoids, helping protect your eyes and heart. Grilling the polenta brings out the sweet corn flavor and adds appealing textural grill marks.

1 cup (5 oz/155 g) polenta
1 Tbsp butter, melted
Salt and freshly ground pepper
1 lb (500 g) asparagus, trimmed
1 pint (6 oz/185 g) cherry tomatoes
2 Tbsp olive oil, plus more for brushing
1 tsp balsamic vinegar
3 Tbsp freshly grated Parmesan cheese

Preheat the oven to 350°F (180°C). In a bowl, combine the polenta, butter, and a large pinch of salt with 3¼ cups (26 fl oz/810 ml) warm water. Pour into an 8-inch (20-cm) square baking dish. Bake the polenta until firm, about 55 minutes. Remove from the oven and let cool to room temperature.

Raise the oven temperature to 500°F (260°C).

Toss the asparagus and cherry tomatoes with the oil and balsamic vinegar and arrange in a single layer on a baking sheet. Season with salt and pepper. Roast just until the tomatoes split and the asparagus is fork-tender, about 10 minutes.

Warm a stove-top grill pan over high heat. Cut the polenta into 8 equal portions and brush both sides of the polenta with oil. Grill until well grill-marked and heated through, about 3 minutes per side.

Divide the grilled polenta among 4 plates, top each with one quarter of the asparagus, cherry tomatoes, and Parmesan, and serve.

ROASTED TOMATO-BASIL SOUP

serves 4

MAY

Tomatoes are rich in vitamins A and C and carotenoids, believed to protect against heart disease and cancer. Roasting the tomatoes and garlic infuses deep flavor into this simple soup. Serve with crusty whole-wheat bread.

10 plum tomatoes, halved lengthwise
4 cloves garlic, minced
4 Tbsp chopped fresh basil
3 Tbsp olive oil
1½ cups (12 fl oz/375 ml) dry white wine
Salt and freshly ground pepper

Preheat the oven to 400°F (200°C). Arrange the tomatoes cut side up and the garlic in a roasting pan. Sprinkle with 1 Tbsp of the basil and drizzle with the oil. Roast until the tomatoes are soft, about 40 minutes. Remove and discard the skins.

In a saucepan over medium-high heat, add the tomatoes, garlic, wine, and ½ cup (4 fl oz/125 ml) water and bring to a boil. Reduce the heat to medium-low and simmer until thickened, about 20 minutes. Season with salt and pepper. Purée the soup in a blender, then reheat in the pan. Serve garnished with the remaining 3 Tbsp basil.

SPANISH GARLIC SHRIMP

serves 4–6

MAY

Inspired by a Spanish-style tapa, this dish requires few ingredients and cooks in a flash. Serve with grilled whole-grain bread to dip in the sauce along with a green salad.

3 Tbsp extra-virgin olive oil
6 cloves garlic, thinly sliced
Pinch of red pepper flakes
1¼ lb (625 g) shrimp, peeled and deveined
½ tsp smoked Spanish paprika
⅓ cup (3 fl oz/80 ml) dry sherry
Salt and fresh ground pepper
1½ tsp chopped fresh flat-leaf parsley

In a large frying pan over medium-high heat, warm the oil. Add the garlic and red pepper flakes and sauté for 15 seconds. Add the shrimp and paprika and sauté until the shrimp curl and turn pink, about 3 minutes. Add the sherry and cook until the sherry is reduced by half, about 1 minute. Season with salt and pepper. Transfer the shrimp and the juices to a serving dish, garnish with the parsley, and serve.

The first days of summer bring sunshine, and as a result, some of the freshest produce available all year. This is the season for making vegetable-centric meals, which are both nutritious and versatile. For balanced meals that come together effortlessly, mix and match your favorite vegetables, and add in whatever whole grains or leftover healthy proteins you have on hand.

june

1

Here, halibut is steamed in a parchment packet, allowing the flavors of lime, garlic, jalapeno, and white wine to absorb into the fish. A small amount of oil tops slivered fresh vegetables to provide richness and nutrients to the dish. Fillets of trout, baby coho salmon, or red snapper can be used instead of halibut.

HALIBUT BAKED IN PARCHMENT

serves 4

2 Tbsp fresh lime juice

1 green onion, thinly sliced

2 cloves garlic, minced

1 small jalapeño chile, seeded and minced

Salt and freshly ground pepper

1 large carrot, coarsely grated

2 leeks, white and tender green parts, cut into fine julienne

2 celery stalks, cut into fine julienne

2 Tbsp chopped fresh flat-leaf parsley

2 Tbsp (2 oz/60 g) extra-virgin olive oil

4 halibut fillets, each 6–8 oz (185–250 g) and 1 inch (2.5 cm) thick

4 Tbsp (2 fl oz/60 ml) dry white wine

Preheat the oven to 425°F (220°C). Cut 4 pieces of parchment paper, each about 12 by 18 inch (30 by 45 cm). Lay the pieces on a work surface. In a small bowl, mix together the lime juice, green onion, garlic, jalapeño, and salt and pepper to taste. In a medium bowl, mix together the carrot, leeks, celery, and parsley.

Sprinkle a few drops of oil in the center of each piece of parchment. Lay 1 fish fillet on each piece of paper, slightly off center. Drizzle the lime juice mixture over the fish, dividing evenly. Place the vegetables on top, dividing evenly. Sprinkle with salt and pepper, the remaining oil, and the wine, again dividing evenly. Fold the parchment in half over the fish by bringing the short sides together and folding them to seal. Fold in the sides so that none of the juices or steam can escape. Place the packets on a baking sheet and bake until the paper is nicely puffed up and starting to brown, about 20 minutes.

Place the packets on warmed individual plates. Carefully slit an X in the top of each packet to let the steam escape and serve.

The steak in this salad can be grilled a day ahead of time and makes for excellent leftovers in sandwiches and stir-fries. This salad features shallots, so thinly sliced they provide a raw crunch that's not too sharp. Try adding sliced pears or apples to this salad for an added element of freshness.

FLANK STEAK SALAD WITH ARUGULA & BLUE CHEESE

serves 4

2 Tbsp extra-virgin olive oil

2 Tbsp sherry vinegar

1 clove garlic, pressed

2 tsp cumin

2 tsp ground coriander

1 lb (500 g) flank steak

Salt and freshly ground pepper

2 cups (2 oz/60 g) arugula

¼ cup (1 oz/30 g) crumbled blue cheese

2 shallots, thinly sliced

2 Tbsp fresh flat-leaf parsley leaves

In a small bowl, whisk together the oil, vinegar, garlic, cumin, and coriander. Place the steak on a plate. Spoon half of the dressing over both sides of the steak, reserving the remaining dressing. Sprinkle both sides of the steak with salt and pepper. Let stand at room temperature for 15 minutes.

Prepare a grill for direct-heat cooking over medium heat. Grill the steak directly over the fire, turning once, until seared on both sides and medium-rare inside, about 8 minutes.

Transfer the steak to a cutting board and let rest for at least 5 minutes. In a bowl, combine the arugula, blue cheese, shallots, and parsley, and drizzle the remaining dressing over the top. Season with salt and pepper and toss together well. Slice the steak, arrange the slices on a platter, top with the arugula salad, and serve.

3

This hybrid potato-meets-bean salad makes a lovely vegetarian lunch that's as satisfying as it is good for you. The bold flavors of olives, capers, and fresh mint brighten the combination of green beans, potatoes, and chickpeas.

TWO-BEAN & POTATO SALAD

serves 4

Salt and freshly ground pepper

¼ lb (125 g) green beans, trimmed

1¼ (625 g) red-skinned potatoes, quartered

1 Tbsp whole-grain mustard

1 Tbsp red wine vinegar

1 Tbsp extra-virgin olive oil

1 cup (7 oz/220 g) cooked or canned chickpeas, drained and rinsed

1 small red onion, finely chopped

½ cup (¾ oz/20 g) coarsely chopped fresh flat-leaf parsley

½ cup (¾ oz/20 g) coarsely chopped fresh mint

4 Sicilian or other green olives, pitted and coarsely chopped

1 Tbsp capers, rinsed and chopped

Prepare a bowl of ice water. Bring a large pot of water to a boil, add 1 Tbsp salt and the green beans, and cook until bright green and tender-crisp, about 3 minutes. Using a slotted spoon, transfer to the bowl of ice water and let stand for 1–2 minutes. Drain the beans and place in a large bowl. Add the potatoes to the boiling water and cook until just tender, about 10 minutes. Drain and let cool.

In a small bowl, whisk together the mustard, vinegar, 1 tsp salt, and ⅛ tsp pepper. Gradually whisk in the oil until blended.

To the bowl with the green beans, add the chickpeas, onion, parsley, mint, olives, capers, and the cooled potatoes. Pour the dressing over the salad and toss to coat. Let the salad stand for about 15 minutes to blend the flavors, and serve.

4

Creamy coconut milk and pungent, fresh spices are blended to make a delicious marinade for pork tenderloin. The spice-infused meat is then threaded onto skewers with metabolism-boosting sweet potato cubes. Serve this dish with your favorite yogurt-based dipping sauce and a green salad.

SPICY PORK KEBABS

serves 4–6

1 can (14 fl oz/430 ml) coconut milk

1 bunch fresh cilantro

2 cloves garlic, crushed

1 chipotle chile in adobo sauce

1 Tbsp ground coriander

Salt and freshly ground pepper

1 lime wedge

2 pork tenderloins, each 1½ lb (1.5 kg), cut into 1-inch (2.5-cm) cubes

2 sweet potatoes, peeled and cut into 1-inch (2.5-cm) cubes

Oil, for grilling

In a blender or food processor, combine the coconut milk, cilantro, garlic, chile, and coriander. Pulse to combine, and then process until the mixture is smooth. Add 1 tsp pepper and a squeeze of lime juice and process to mix. Taste and add salt and more lime juice, if needed.

Place the pork cubes in a large locking plastic bag and pour in the marinade. Seal the bag, massage the marinade around the meat, and refrigerate for at least 4 hours or up to overnight. At least 30 minutes before you plan to begin grilling, remove the pork from the refrigerator. Discard the marinade. If using wooden skewers, soak them in water for at least 30 minutes.

In a large pot, combine the sweet potato cubes with water to cover. Bring to a boil over high heat and cook for 5 minutes. Drain and let cool.

Prepare a grill for direct-heat cooking over high heat. Brush and oil the grill grate. Thread the pork and sweet potato cubes onto the skewers, leaving some space between the cubes. Grill the skewers until nicely grill-marked, about 5 minutes. Turn the skewers and cook for about 5 minutes longer. The pork should feel just firm to the touch (for medium), and the sweet potato cubes should be tender.

Transfer the skewers to a platter and let rest for 5 minutes. Slide the pork and sweet potato cubes off the skewers onto a platter, and serve.

PASTA WITH ROSEMARY-LAMB SUGO

serves 4

2 Tbsp olive oil

1 large onion, thinly sliced

1 Tbsp minced fresh rosemary

½ lb (500 g) ground lamb

Salt and freshly ground pepper

¼ cup (2 fl oz/60 ml) dry white wine

2 cans (14.5 oz/455 g each) diced tomatoes

2 large zucchini, cut into ½-inch (12-mm) cubes

12 oz (375 g) rotini pasta, preferably multigrain

¼ cup (1 oz/30 g) grated pecorino romano cheese, plus more for serving

Sugo is Italian for juice, but here it refers to a rustic ragu of ground lamb, cubed zucchini, and lots of Mediterranean flavors. This infused sauce is delicious mixed into curly, multigrain rotini pasta. Basil would make an equally delicious replacement for the rosemary. Just substitute 3 Tbsp chopped fresh basil when adding the cheese.

In a large frying pan over medium-high heat, warm the oil. Add the onion and rosemary and sauté until the onion is tender, about 5 minutes. Add the lamb and sprinkle with salt and pepper. Sauté until the lamb is no longer pink, breaking up the meat with a wooden spoon, about 3 minutes. Add the wine and boil until absorbed, about 2 minutes. Add the tomatoes with their juices, and bring to a boil. Stir in the zucchini. Reduce the heat to medium-low and boil until the sauce is thick, stirring occasionally, about 10 minutes.

Meanwhile, bring a large pot of salted water to a boil. Add the pasta, stir well, and cook until al dente, about 11 minutes, or according to package directions. Drain the pasta, and then add to the sauce and toss to coat. Mix in the ¼ cup (1 oz/30 g) cheese.

Taste and adjust the seasoning. Transfer to warmed shallow bowls and serve, passing additional cheese at the table.

SEA BASS IN PARCHMENT WITH SALSA VERDE

serves 6

6 sea bass fillets, each 5–6 oz (155–185 g) and about ¾ inch (2 cm) thick, skinned

Salt

½ lb (250 g) tomatillos, husked and rinsed, then coarsely chopped

2 bunches fresh cilantro, large stems removed, coarsely chopped

1 bunch fresh flat-leaf parsley, large stems removed, coarsely chopped

3 fresh mint sprigs, coarsely chopped

3 jalapeño chiles, coarsely chopped

5 cloves garlic, coarsely chopped

¼ white onion, coarsely chopped

¾ cup (6 fl oz/180 ml) dry white wine

⅓ cup (3 fl oz/80 ml) extra-virgin olive oil

Vibrant and nutrient-packed salsa verde, which literally translates to green sauce, infuses sea bass with tangy tomatillo and spicy jalapeño flavors. Any leftover salsa is delicious served with grilled meat or fish. Accompany this dish with steamed brown rice.

Preheat the oven to 450°F (230°C). Sprinkle the fish on both sides with salt.

In a blender, combine the tomatillos, cilantro, parsley, mint, chiles, garlic, onion, and wine and blend until very smooth and thick. Season to taste with salt.

Cut 8 pieces of parchment paper, each about 12 by 18 inches (30 by 45 cm). Lay the pieces on a work surface. Brush the center of each sheet with some of the oil. Spoon 3 Tbsp of the sauce slightly off center on one half of each sheet of parchment, place a fillet on top of the sauce, and rub the fish generously with the remaining oil, dividing it evenly. Cover with another ½ cup (4 fl oz/125 ml) of the sauce, making certain it does not come close to the edge of the parchment. Fold the parchment in half over the fish by bringing the short sides together and folding them to seal. Fold in the sides so that none of the juices or steam can escape. Place the packets on a baking sheet and place in the oven. Bake until the paper begins to brown and puff, 10–15 minutes. Remove from the oven and let stand for 5 minutes.

Place the packets on warmed plates. Carefully slit an X in the top of each packet to let the steam escape, and serve.

7

BAKED EGGS IN SPICY TOMATO-PEPPER SAUCE

serves 4

In this simple Cuban classic, baked eggs are nestled in a thick, savory sauce of peppers and tomatoes, and topped with a heady drizzle of olive oil and sherry. The dish can be made and served in one pan or in individual baking dishes.

2 Tbsp canola oil

1 large white onion, diced

4 cloves garlic, minced

1 large green bell pepper, seeded and diced

2 plum tomatoes, diced, or 1 cup (6 oz/185 g) drained, canned, and diced tomatoes

½ cup (3 oz/90 g) jarred diced red pimientos, drained

4 Tbsp (2 fl oz/60 ml) dry sherry

Salt and freshly ground pepper

8 large eggs

Extra-virgin olive oil for drizzling

Position a rack in the upper third of the oven and preheat to 350°F (180°C). In a shallow 10-inch (25-cm) enameled cast iron pan or other nonreactive flameproof pan over medium heat, warm the oil. Add the onion and garlic and cook, stirring, until translucent, 2–3 minutes. Add the bell pepper and cook, stirring, until beginning to soften, about 2 minutes. Stir in the tomatoes and cook until the mixture forms a thick, juicy sauce, about 15 minutes. Set aside 1 Tbsp of the pimientos and add the rest to the sauce. Add 3 Tbsp of the sherry, stir to mix well, and cook until heated through, about 2 minutes. Stir in 1 tsp salt and ½ tsp pepper.

Crack the eggs and arrange on top of the sauce, spacing them evenly in the pan. Drizzle the eggs with the remaining 1 Tbsp sherry, sprinkle with a little more salt and pepper, and top each egg with a drizzle of olive oil and some of the reserved pimiento. Bake, uncovered, until the eggs are done to your liking, about 10 minutes for a soft to runny yolk or 15 minutes for a hard-cooked yolk. Serve from the pan.

8

STEAK KEBABS WITH SPICY GINGER-LIME SAUCE

serves 2

The low-fat marinade for these kebabs combines the flavors of classic Asian and South American dishes. Try threading some 1-inch (2.5 cm) cubes of red or yellow bell peppers onto the skewers for added nutrients.

¼ cup (2 fl oz/60 ml) fresh lime juice, plus lime wedges for garnish

3 Tbsp vegetable oil

1 Tbsp low-sodium soy sauce

1 Tbsp fresh ginger, minced

1 small shallot, minced

1 serrano chile, seeded and minced

1 tsp sugar

8–10 oz (250–315 g) skirt steak

2 Tbsp minced fresh cilantro

1 Tbsp minced fresh mint

Salt and freshly ground pepper

Hot cooked brown jasmine or basmati rice for serving

Soak 8 wooden skewers in water for 30 minutes. Meanwhile, in a small bowl, combine the lime juice, 2 Tbsp of the oil, the soy sauce, ginger, shallot, chile, sugar, and 2 Tbsp water to make a dipping sauce.

Cut the steak crosswise into strips 3 inches (7.5 cm) long, and then cut each strip in half crosswise. You should have 16 pieces. Place the steak pieces in a medium bowl, add 2 Tbsp of the dipping sauce and the remaining 1 Tbsp oil, and stir to coat. Let the steak marinate for 10–15 minutes. Mix the cilantro and mint into the remaining dipping sauce.

Prepare a grill for direct-heat cooking over high heat. Thread 2 pieces of steak onto each skewer and season with salt and pepper. Grill the skewers to the desired doneness, about 3 minutes on each side for rare.

To serve, pass the skewers with the rice, dipping sauce, and lime wedges.

9

GRILLED VEGETABLE GYROS WITH CUCUMBER-MINT SAUCE

serves 4–6

A gyro is a Greek dish of lamb roasted on a vertical spit. Since Greek-style spice blends really pack a flavor punch, you won't miss the meat with this all-vegetable spin on the traditional dish. This medley of brightly colored vegetables offers an abundance of vitamins and minerals and looks beautiful when served buffet style. If you don't have access to a grill, you can also use a stove-top grill pan.

2 tsp salt

2 tsp chili powder

1 tsp *each* ground cumin, garlic powder, dried oregano, and dried thyme

½ tsp ground cinnamon

1 zucchini, halved lengthwise and thinly sliced

1 red pepper, seeds and ribs removed, and sliced

1 yellow pepper, seeds and ribs removed, and sliced

1 yellow onion, halved and thinly sliced

½ lb (250 g) mushrooms, halved

2 Tbsp olive oil

FOR THE CUCUMBER-MINT SAUCE

2 cups (16 oz/500 g) plain Greek yogurt

1 cucumber, peeled, seeded and chopped

2 cloves garlic

2 Tbsp chopped fresh mint

2 Tbsp fresh lemon juice

Salt and freshly ground pepper

6 whole-wheat pitas, cut in half and split open to form pockets

Combine the salt, chili powder, cumin, garlic powder, oregano, thyme, and cinnamon in a large bowl. Add the zucchini, peppers, onion, mushrooms, and the oil and toss to combine. Set aside.

To make the sauce, in a food processor, combine the yogurt, cucumber, garlic, mint, and lemon juice and process until smooth. Season with salt and pepper and set aside.

Prepare a grill for direct-heat cooking over high heat. Place the reserved vegetables in a grill basket and place on the grill. Cook, stirring occasionally, until the vegetables are fork-tender and browned all over, about 12 minutes.

Divide the vegetables among the pita pockets and drizzle with a generous helping of the sauce. Serve, passing extra sauce at the table.

10

CHICKEN-VEGETABLE SAUTÉ WITH LEMON & TARRAGON

serves 2

Low-sodium chicken broth serves as the base of this healthy, yet creamy, lemon tarragon sauce that tops quick-cooking chicken tenders. Serve this dish with fluffy quinoa or whole-wheat orzo.

All-purpose flour, for dredging

10 oz (315 g) chicken breast tenders

Salt and freshly ground pepper

2 Tbsp olive oil

½ lb (250 g) thin asparagus, ends trimmed

½ lb (250 g) sugar snap peas, strings removed

1 cup (8 fl oz/250 ml) low-sodium chicken broth

1 Tbsp minced fresh chives, plus more for garnish

2 tsp minced fresh tarragon, plus more for garnish

2 Tbsp fresh lemon juice

Spread the flour on a plate. Cut the chicken tenders in half crosswise. Sprinkle them with salt and pepper, then dredge in the flour.

In a large frying pan over medium-high heat, warm 1 Tbsp of the oil. Add the chicken and sauté until just cooked through, about 5 minutes. Transfer to a plate. Add the remaining 1 Tbsp oil to the frying pan, and reduce the heat to medium. Add the asparagus and sauté for 1 minute. Add the sugar snap peas; raise the heat to medium-high. Season the vegetables with salt and pepper and sauté for 1 minute. Add the broth and bring to a boil, stirring up the browned bits on the pan bottom. Cover the pan and boil until the vegetables are almost tender-crisp, about 3 minutes.

Return the chicken to the pan. Add half each of the tarragon and chives and the lemon juice. Simmer uncovered until the sauce thickens and coats the chicken, stirring almost constantly, about 2 minutes. Taste and adjust the seasoning.

Divide the chicken and vegetables between 2 warmed plates, garnish with the remaining tarragon and chives, and serve.

Apricot season is short but it's worth seeking them out for this dish. The apricot chutney comes together in under 10 minutes, and incorporates such a vibrant array of flavors, you may never go back to the store-bought version.

GRILLED PORK WITH FRESH APRICOT CHUTNEY

serves 6

FOR THE APRICOT CHUTNEY

1 Tbsp coriander seeds

¼ cup (1 oz/30 g) sliced shallots

2 Tbsp packed brown sugar

1 Tbsp cider vinegar

1 cinnamon stick

Pinch of red pepper flakes

1½ lb (750 g) apricots, pitted and diced

1 Tbsp honey

¼ tsp salt

2 Tbsp chopped fresh cilantro

2 Tbsp chopped fresh mint

1 pork tenderloin, about 1¼ lb (625 g)

1 Tbsp Asian sesame oil

1 Tbsp coriander seeds, lightly crushed

½ tsp salt

1½ Tbsp honey

To make the chutney, in a small frying pan over medium heat, lightly toast the coriander seeds, about 1 minute. Set aside. In a saucepan over medium heat, combine the shallots, brown sugar, vinegar, cinnamon stick, pepper flakes, and 2 Tbsp water, and bring to a simmer. Simmer until the shallot is tender and the mixture is syrupy, about 2 minutes. Stir in the apricots and toasted coriander seeds and cook until the apricots are just tender, about 3 minutes. Remove from the heat and stir in the honey and salt. Let cool completely, then stir in the cilantro and mint.

Prepare a grill for direct-heat cooking over medium-high heat. Brush the pork on all sides with the sesame oil, then coat evenly with the crushed coriander seeds and salt. Grill the pork, turning frequently, until well browned on all sides, about 12 minutes total.

Spread the honey over the surface of the pork and continue to grill until an instant-read thermometer inserted into the thickest part of the tenderloin registers 140°F (60°C) and the pork is nicely glazed, about 4 minutes longer. Transfer the pork to a platter, let it rest for 5 minutes, then cut into thin slices and serve with the chutney.

Serve these healthy quesadillas with a quick homemade salsa: In a bowl, combine 1 tomato, seeded and diced; ½ white onion, diced; 2 Tbsp chopped fresh cilantro, and ½ jalapeño chile, seeded and minced. Add lime juice, salt, and pepper to taste and toss gently.

VEGETABLE QUESADILLAS

serves 4

½ cup (4 fl oz/125 ml) dry white wine

¼ cup (2 fl oz/60 ml) olive oil

Salt and freshly ground pepper

1 small eggplant, cut into chunks

2 zucchini, cut into chunks

2 yellow squash, cut into chunks

1 red onion, quartered lengthwise and separated into double-thick wedges

1 red bell pepper, seeded and cut into large pieces

8 corn tortillas, 8 inches (20 cm) in diameter

1 cup (4 oz/125 g) shredded pepper jack or Monterey jack cheese

Canola oil, for brushing

3 Tbsp coarsely chopped fresh cilantro

Prepare a grill for direct-heat cooking over high heat. In a large bowl, whisk together the wine, oil, ½ tsp salt, and ½ tsp pepper. Add the eggplant, squashes, onion, and bell pepper, and toss gently to coat.

When the grill is ready, place all the vegetables in a grill basket and place on the grill. Cook, stirring occasionally, until the vegetables are fork-tender and browned all over, about 12 minutes. Transfer the vegetables to a cutting board, let cool slightly, and then chop into small pieces.

Spread out the tortillas on a work surface. Distribute half of the cheese and chopped vegetables on 2 of the tortillas, dividing evenly. Top each one with another tortilla, and press firmly. Stack the quesadillas on a plate and set aside. Preheat the oven to 200°F (95°C).

Warm 2 frying pans over medium heat until hot. Brush the pans lightly with the oil. Place a quesadilla in each pan and cook, turning once, until lightly toasted, about 2 minutes on each side. Transfer to a baking sheet and keep warm in the oven. Repeat with the remaining tortillas, cheese, and vegetables, brushing the pan with oil. Cut the quesadillas into wedges, sprinkle with the cilantro, and serve.

13

SESAME-CRUSTED SALMON WITH CHERMOULA

serves 4

4 Tbsp (4 fl oz/60 ml) extra-virgin olive oil, plus more for drizzling

½ cup (3 oz/90 g) minced shallot

½ cup (2½ oz/75 g) chopped red bell pepper

3 cloves garlic, chopped

1 tsp *each* ground cumin, ground coriander, and paprika

Salt and freshly ground pepper

¼ tsp red pepper flakes, plus more if desired

Leaves from 1 bunch fresh flat-leaf parsley, chopped

Leaves from 1 bunch fresh cilantro, chopped

Grated zest and juice of 1 lemon

4 skin-on salmon fillets, each about 6 oz (185 g)

¼ cup (1 oz/30 g) black sesame seeds

Sesame seeds are a great source of copper, an anti-inflammatory mineral, and they make a wonderful crisp coating for pan-seared salmon. Black sesame seeds add a striking color contrast, but the white variety will work just fine too. Serve with a side of sautéed chard or spinach.

To make the chermoula, warm a sauté pan over medium-high heat and add 2 Tbsp oil. When the oil is hot, add the shallot and bell pepper. Sauté for about 3 minutes or until the vegetables begin to soften. Add the garlic, cumin, coriander, paprika, ½ tsp salt, and the red pepper flakes. Sauté for 1 minute or until the garlic is fragrant. Transfer the contents of the pan to a food processor. Add the parsley, cilantro, and lemon zest and juice to the vegetables and pulse the mixture about 10 times or until blended but still slightly chunky. Scrape down the sides and pulse a few more times. Taste and adjust the seasoning with more salt or pepper flakes.

Arrange the salmon fillets skin-side down on a cutting board. Pat them dry and season with salt and pepper. Drizzle the fillets with a drop of oil, coating them with your fingers. Sprinkle the sesame seeds on top and press lightly to adhere.

Warm a large sauté pan over medium-high heat and add the remaining 2 Tbsp oil to the pan. When the oil is hot, add the salmon, sesame seed–side down. Turn the fish after 3 minutes. The sesame seeds should be crisp. Cook the second side for another 3 minutes or until cooked through.

Transfer the fillets to warmed plates and serve with a dollop of chermoula.

14

GRILLED POLENTA WITH BLACK BEAN SALSA

serves 6

Salt

1⅓ cups (9½ oz/295 g) coarse-ground polenta

1 can (15 oz/485 g) black beans, drained and rinsed

1 large ripe tomato, seeded and diced

½ cup (3 oz/90 g) fresh corn kernels

¼ cup (1½ oz/45 g) minced yellow onion

3 Tbsp chopped fresh cilantro

1 Tbsp fresh lime juice

1 jalapeño chile, seeded and minced

1 clove garlic, minced

1 Tbsp olive oil

½ cup (2½ oz/75 g) crumbled queso fresco or feta cheese for serving

Smooth creamy polenta makes the perfect base for a crunchy vegetable salsa. Fresh corn adds texture and sweetness, and black beans contribute protein and fiber. This salsa is also delicious with tortilla chips or served on grilled chicken.

To make the polenta, in a large, heavy saucepan, bring 5⅓ cups (43 fl oz/1.3 l) water and 1½ tsp salt to a boil over medium-high heat. Gradually whisk in the polenta. Reduce the heat to medium-low and cover. Cook, whisking frequently, until the polenta is thick, about 45 minutes. Add up to ½ cup (4 fl oz/125 ml) water by tablespoons if the polenta begins to stick to the bottom of the pan.

Lightly oil a 9-by-13-inch (23-by-33-cm) baking dish. Spread the polenta in the dish. Cover the polenta with parchment or waxed paper and refrigerate until firm and cold, at least 1½ hours or up to overnight.

To make the salsa, in a bowl, stir together the beans, tomato, corn, onion, cilantro, lime juice, chile, and garlic. Season with salt. Cover and let stand for at least 30 minutes.

Preheat the broiler. Have ready a rimmed baking sheet. Cut the polenta crosswise into 6 rectangles, and brush the tops with half of the oil. Using a wide spatula, transfer the polenta pieces to the baking sheet, oiled sides down. Brush with the remaining oil. Broil, turning once, until both sides are golden, about 5 minutes per side.

Cut each rectangle into 3 triangles. Arrange 3 triangles on each plate, and top with the salsa, dividing it evenly. Sprinkle with the cheese, and serve.

15

ROASTED SUMMER VEGETABLE SALAD WITH GOAT CHEESE

serves 4

This Mediterranean-inspired salad features the best of summer produce, roasted until tender and caramelized. The vegetables are then mixed with crunchy fresh lettuce and tossed with a light sherry vinaigrette for an appealing contrast of textures and flavors. A small amount of goat cheese lends a tangy richness without a lot of added fat. If you have it, toss in some leftover cooked quinoa or barley.

1 lb (500 g) yellow or red bell peppers, seeded

1 lb (500 g) Asian eggplants

1 red onion

½ lb (250 g) zucchini

4 Tbsp (2 fl oz/60 ml) olive oil

3 cloves garlic, minced

¾ tsp ground cumin

¾ tsp smoked paprika

Salt and freshly ground pepper

3 Tbsp sherry vinegar or red wine vinegar

1 head red leaf lettuce, separated into leaves

4 oz (125 g) fresh goat cheese, crumbled

Preheat the oven to 400°F (200°C). Cut the bell peppers, eggplant, onion, and zucchini into 1-inch (2.5-cm) pieces.

Pour 2 Tbsp oil into a large roasting pan. Add the vegetables, sprinkle with the garlic, cumin, paprika, ¾ tsp salt, and ¼ tsp pepper, and stir to combine. Roast, stirring every 10 minutes, until tender, about 25 minutes. Drizzle with 1 Tbsp of the vinegar and season to taste.

In a bowl, whisk together the remaining 2 Tbsp vinegar and 2 Tbsp oil. Add the lettuce leaves and toss to coat. Divide the lettuce among 4 plates, stacking the leaves slightly to make a bed for the vegetables. Spoon the vegetables evenly over the lettuce, dividing evenly. Sprinkle about 2 Tbsp goat cheese over each salad, and serve.

16

SPICY CHICKEN & BASIL STIR-FRY

serves 4

The Thai basil featured in this zesty stir-fry has a complex flavor composed of citrus, anise, and mint notes. The herb is rich in antimicrobial and anti-inflammatory benefits. Serve over brown rice or stir into buckwheat noodles.

6 Tbsp (3 fl oz/90 ml) low-sodium chicken broth

2 Tbsp Asian fish sauce

2 tsp light brown sugar

½ teaspoon cornstarch

2 Tbsp canola oil

1 large red bell pepper, seeded and cut into strips ¼ inch (6 mm) wide

1 or 2 jalapeño chiles, cut crosswise into very thin slices

2 cloves garlic, minced

4 skinless, boneless chicken breast halves, about 1 lb (500 g) total weight, cut across the grain into thin strips

¾ cup (1 oz/30 g) thinly sliced fresh Thai basil

3 green onions, cut into 3-inch (7.5-cm) lengths

Hot cooked brown rice, for serving

In a small bowl, whisk together the broth, fish sauce, and brown sugar. Add the cornstarch and whisk until the cornstarch and sugar are dissolved to make a sauce.

Warm a wok or large frying pan over high heat and add the oil. Add the bell pepper and stir-fry for 1 minute. Add the chile and the garlic and stir-fry until fragrant, about 20 seconds. Add the chicken strips and stir-fry until the chicken loses its pink color, 2–3 minutes. Stir in the basil and green onions and stir-fry until the green onions are barely wilted, about 1 minute.

Whisk the sauce and pour it into the pan. Cook just until the liquid comes to a boil. Serve over rice.

17

LAMB BURGERS WITH SPINACH & SPICED YOGURT SAUCE

serves 4

¾ cup (3¾ oz/110 g) red onion, finely chopped

½ cup (4 oz/125 g) plain whole-milk yogurt

½ tsp ground cumin

Pinch of cayenne pepper

Salt and freshly ground pepper

1¼ lb (625 g) ground lamb

¾ tsp ground allspice

Olive oil, for brushing

4 whole-wheat buns

1 tomato, sliced

4 handfuls baby spinach leaves

Lean ground lamb is a novel alternative to beef in these spiced burgers. Ditch the buns for a gluten-free option, and double the amount of spinach to serve the burgers on a bed of greens. Yogurt adds creaminess and protein in the slightly spicy sauce.

In a small bowl, mix ¼ cup (1 oz/30 g) of the onion with the yogurt, cumin, and cayenne. Season with salt and pepper and set aside.

In a bowl, combine the lamb and allspice with the remaining onion, 1 tsp salt, and a generous amount of pepper. Mix gently to blend. Form the lamb mixture into 4 patties, each ½-inch (12-mm) thick. Heat a large frying pan over medium-high heat; brush with oil. Add the lamb patties and cook to the desired doneness, about 5 minutes per side for medium.

Meanwhile, preheat the broiler. Brush the cut surface of the buns with oil, then broil, oiled side up, until beginning to brown, about 2 minutes. Divide the bun bottoms among 4 warmed plates. Top each with a patty.

Spoon some of the yogurt sauce over each patty, top with a couple slices of tomato and a handful of spinach leaves and top with the bun tops. Serve, passing additional sauce at the table.

18

ITALIAN SHELLFISH STEW

serves 4

2 Tbsp extra-virgin olive oil

1 large yellow onion, chopped

1 clove garlic, minced

8 plum tomatoes, halved lengthwise, seeded, and diced

¼ tsp red pepper flakes

½ cup (4 fl oz/125 ml) tomato sauce

½ cup (4 fl oz/125 ml) dry red wine

¾ lb (375 g) cleaned squid, tentacles trimmed, bodies cut in ½-inch (12-mm) rings

¾ lb (375 g) firm white fish fillet, cut into ¾-inch (2-cm) pieces

½ lb (250 g) sea scallops, side muscle removed, halved horizontally

¼ lb (125 g) shrimp, peeled and deveined

12 littleneck clams, well scrubbed

4 slices coarse country whole-wheat bread, each about 1 inch (2.5 cm) thick, toasted

2 cloves garlic, halved lengthwise

Chopped fresh flat-leaf parsley

Shellfish are a source of lean protein, omega-3 fatty acids, and minerals, and they cook quickly in this tomato-based stew. Their porous texture picks up the flavors of garlic, red pepper flakes, and red wine. This dish makes for a quick and low-calorie lunch.

In a large Dutch oven or other deep, heavy pot over medium-high heat, warm the oil. Add the onion and garlic and sauté until the onion is soft, about 4 minutes. Add the tomatoes and red pepper flakes and sauté until the tomatoes soften, about 5 minutes. Pour in the tomato sauce and wine, bring to a boil, reduce the heat to medium, cover, and cook for 10 minutes.

Add the squid, re-cover, and simmer for 10 minutes. Add the white fish, scallops, and shrimp, re-cover, and cook until the shrimp and scallops are opaque throughout but still tender, about 10 minutes. Add the clams, discarding any that do not close to the touch, cover, and cook just until they open, 4–5 minutes. Discard any clams that failed to open.

Rub each bread slice generously on one side with a garlic clove half. Place each slice, garlic side up, in a warmed wide, shallow soup bowl. Ladle one-fourth of the stew into each bowl, dividing the fish and shellfish evenly. Garnish with the parsley, and serve.

19

JUNE

Spicy marinated steak is tucked into warm gluten-free tortillas and topped with a fresh salsa for a healthy meal that pleases many palates. Chipotles add a smoky warmth to salsa and are rich in capsaicin, known to improve digestion. If you like, add some shredded red cabbage to the tacos for added texture and fiber.

GRILLED STEAK TACOS WITH CHIPOTLE SALSA & AVOCADO

serves 4–6

½ cup (4 fl oz/125 ml) canola oil

1 yellow onion, thinly sliced

2 cloves garlic, chopped

1 jalapeño chile, seeded and minced

1 Tbsp chopped fresh oregano

1 tsp ground cumin

1 Tbsp ancho chile powder

2 Tbsp chopped fresh cilantro

1 Tbsp tequila

Salt

1 flank steak, 2½–3 lb (1–1.5 kg), trimmed of fat and silver skin

FOR THE CHIPOTLE SALSA

2 cloves garlic, unpeeled

2 ripe tomatoes, about 1 lb (500 g)

3 chipotle chiles in adobo

Salt

Oil, for grilling

12 corn tortillas

2 avocados, peeled, halved, and thinly sliced

In a small bowl, mix together the oil, onion, garlic, jalapeño, oregano, cumin, chile powder, cilantro, tequila, and 1½ tsp salt. Score the steak a few times across the grain. Put the steak in a baking dish and pour over the marinade. Cover and let marinate in the refrigerator, turning occasionally, for at least 6 hours or up to overnight. Remove from the refrigerator 30 minutes before grilling.

To make the salsa, preheat the broiler and line a small rimmed baking sheet with foil. Arrange the garlic and tomatoes on the baking sheet and place under the broiler. Broil until the vegetable skins are blackened on all sides, turning with tongs as they char, about 5 minutes for the garlic and 10–15 minutes for the tomatoes. Set aside to cool. Peel the garlic and add it to a blender along with the tomatoes (you do not need to peel the charred tomato skin) and chiles. Process briefly, until the mixture is thick but still chunky. Pour the salsa into a bowl, season with salt, cover, and let stand at room temperature for 20–30 minutes. ⤳

Prepare a grill for direct-heat cooking over high heat. Generously oil the grill rack. Preheat the oven to 200°F (95°C).

Remove the steak from the marinade, pat dry, and discard the marinade. Grill the steak directly over the heat, turning once, until well-browned and medium-rare in the center, 9–10 minutes. (Move the steak to a cooler part of the grill if flare-ups occur.) The steak should not be cooked past medium-rare, as it will toughen. Transfer the meat to a platter, cover loosely with foil, and let rest for about 15 minutes.

Quickly grill the tortillas and then divide into two equal stacks. Wrap each stack tightly in foil. Place the tortillas in the oven and keep warm.

Slice the steak thinly against the grain.

To assemble the tacos, place the steak on one side of the tortilla, spoon a little salsa and avocado on top, fold, and serve.

20

JUNE

This protein-rich salad couldn't be any easier: just rinse, chop, and mix for a healthy salad that's perfect for a busy day.

SOUTHWESTERN BEAN SALAD

serves 4

2 cans (15 oz/470 g each) black beans

1 can (15 oz/470 g) red kidney beans

2 ears grilled husked corn

1 cup (6 oz/185 g) prepared pico de gallo

2 green onions, thinly sliced

½ cup (¾ oz/20 g) chopped fresh cilantro

Juice of 1 lime

Salt and freshly ground pepper

Drain and rinse the beans. Stand each ear of corn upright on a cutting board and, using a large sharp knife, cut the kernels from the cob. Transfer the kernels to a bowl and add the beans, pico de gallo, and green onions. Stir to mix. Stir in the cilantro, then season with the lime juice, salt, and pepper. Serve at room temperature, or cover and refrigerate for about 2 hours and serve chilled.

21

Pistou, the French version of pesto, is lower in fat than the classic version because it doesn't contain pine nuts. It makes a healthy and flavor-packed addition to vegetable soups.

VEGETABLE SOUP WITH PISTOU

serves 6

½ lb (250 g) fresh cranberry beans, shelled

6 fresh thyme sprigs

4 fresh flat-leaf parsley sprigs

1 dried bay leaf

1 red onion, diced

1 celery stalk, sliced

1 zucchini, quartered lengthwise, and sliced

1 ripe tomato, seeded, and chopped

¼ lb (125 g) green beans, cut into pieces

1 Yukon gold potato, cut into chunks

2 Tbsp tomato paste

Salt and freshly ground pepper

FOR THE PISTOU

1 cup (1 oz/30 g) lightly packed fresh basil

½ ripe tomato, seeded and chopped

4 cloves garlic, coarsely chopped

½ tsp salt

3 Tbsp extra-virgin olive oil

¼ cup (1 oz/30 g) grated Parmesan cheese

Place the beans in a soup pot, add 6 cups (48 fl oz/1.5 l) cold water, and bring to a boil over high heat. Tie the thyme, parsley, and bay leaf in a square of cheesecloth and add to the pot. Reduce the heat to medium and simmer for 15 minutes. Remove and discard the herb bundle. Add the onion, celery, zucchini, tomato, green beans, and potatoes to the soup and simmer until the beans are soft and the vegetables are crisp-tender, about 15 minutes. Stir in the tomato paste and season with salt and pepper.

To make the pistou, in a food processor, combine the basil, tomato, garlic, and salt and process until finely chopped, about 1 minute, stopping to scrape down the sides of the bowl as needed. With the machine running, add the oil in a slow, steady stream and process until almost smooth. Add the cheese and pulse to blend. Taste and adjust the seasoning.

Ladle the soup into warmed bowls and top with a dollop of the pistou. Serve, passing the remaining pistou at the table.

22

This bulked-up version of fattoush salad includes all the essential ingredients, plus protein, in the form of lean lamb steaks, and extra vegetables. Trim any excess fat off the lamb before cooking to cut down on extra fat calories. After grilling, you can also cut the meat into bite-size pieces and mix them into the salad.

LAMB & PITA SALAD

serves 4–6

1¼ lb (625 g) boneless lamb leg steaks, each about ½ inch (12 mm) thick

2 Tbsp olive oil

½ tsp ground cumin

Salt and freshly ground pepper

FOR THE PITA SALAD

2 whole-wheat pita breads, split horizontally

2 cloves garlic

2 Tbsp fresh lemon juice

2 tsp *each* pomegranate molasses and honey

¼ cup (2 fl oz/60 ml) extra-virgin olive oil

2 large tomatoes, seeded and diced

4 green onions, thinly sliced

1 English cucumber, seeded and diced

4–6 radishes, coarsely chopped

1 head romaine lettuce, pale inner leaves, cut crosswise into ½-inch (12-mm) pieces

½ cup (½ oz/15 g) *each* coarsely chopped fresh flat-leaf parsley and mint

1 Tbsp ground sumac or grated lemon zest

Brush the lamb steaks with oil and season with the cumin and with salt and pepper. Let stand at room temperature for about 1 hour.

To make the pita salad, preheat the oven to 350°F (180°C). Arrange the pita breads on a baking sheet and bake until lightly crisped and golden, about 10 minutes. Let cool, then break into 1-inch (2.5-cm) pieces. In a mini food processor, process the garlic until minced. Add the lemon juice, molasses, honey, oil, and 1 tsp salt. Pulse to combine.

In a large bowl, combine the tomatoes, green onions, cucumber, radishes, lettuce, parsley, and mint. Toss to combine, then refrigerate.

Prepare a grill for direct-heat cooking over high heat. Place the steaks over the hottest part of the fire and cook, turning once, until an instant-read thermometer inserted into a steak registers 135°F (57°C) for medium-rare, 2–2½ minutes per side, or to your desired doneness. Transfer to a cutting board and let rest for 5 minutes. Cut the steaks crosswise into strips 1 inch (2.5 cm) wide.

Add the pita pieces to the salad, drizzle with the dressing, and toss. Arrange the lamb on top, sprinkle with the sumac, and serve.

23

Mint pesto is a pleasant change of pace from the norm of basil. Mint's sweet leaves are known to protect the body from bad bacteria. This healthy and delicious pesto tastes terrific over sautéed carrots and pan-seared chicken.

CHICKEN CUTLETS WITH MINT PESTO & SPICY CARROTS

serves 2

FOR THE MINT PESTO
¼ cup (¼ oz/8 g) packed fresh mint leaves
¼ cup (1 oz/30 g) toasted whole almonds
½ small shallot
¼ cup (2 fl oz/60 ml) extra-virgin olive oil
1½ tsp fresh lemon juice
Salt and freshly ground pepper

2 Tbsp extra-virgin olive oil
¾ lb (375 g) chicken breast cutlets
Salt and freshly ground black pepper
1 shallot, minced
Pinch of red pepper flakes
2 carrots, shredded
2 tsp fresh lemon juice
Chopped fresh mint for garnish

To make the pesto, in a food processor, combine the mint, almonds, and shallot and process until finely ground. With the machine running, gradually add the oil. Mix in the lemon juice, and then season to taste with salt and pepper. Set aside.

In a large frying pan over medium-high heat, warm 1 Tbsp of the oil. Season the chicken with salt and pepper, add to the pan, and sauté until cooked through, 2–3 minutes per side. Transfer the chicken to a warmed plate.

Add the remaining 1 Tbsp oil to the pan, and then add the shallot and pepper flakes. Sauté until the shallot begins to soften, about 1 minute. Add the carrots and sprinkle lightly with salt and pepper. Sauté until the carrots are tender-crisp, 2–3 minutes. Mix in the lemon juice and any juices from the plate holding the chicken. Taste and adjust the seasoning.

Divide the carrots between 2 warmed plates and top with the chicken. Thin the pesto with a little hot water, if desired, and spoon over the chicken. Sprinkle with sliced mint, and serve.

24

Impress guests with this elegant meal that's actually very easy to prepare. A simple pizza is composed with fresh ingredients and a sparse coating of cheese. It's then topped with a mixed spring salad for a 2-in-1 meal. If you want extra protein, leftover shredded pork or chicken would make a delicious addition.

SALAD-TOPPED GRILLED PIZZA

serves 2

Olive oil, for shaping and brushing
1 lb (500 g) purchased whole-wheat pizza dough, at room temperature
All-purpose flour, for dusting
Salt and freshly ground pepper
3 cloves garlic, thinly sliced
2 small plum tomatoes, very thinly sliced
2-oz (125-g) chunk Parmesan cheese, shaved with a vegetable peeler
1 Tbsp balsamic vinegar
1 tsp Dijon mustard
2 Tbsp extra-virgin olive oil
4 cups (4 oz/125 g) loosely packed spring salad greens

Prepare a grill for indirect-heat cooking and oil the grill rack. Turn the dough out onto a lightly floured work surface. Shape it into 2 balls. Cover one of the balls with a clean kitchen towel. With oiled fingers, press the second ball into a 7-inch (18-cm) round of even thickness. Cover the dough round with a clean kitchen towel and let rise for 15 minutes. Meanwhile, shape the second dough round.

Place the first dough round, floured side down, on the oiled, cool part of the grill and close the cover. Cook until the top of the dough bubbles and the bottom is grill-marked, 3–5 minutes. With a long-handled spatula, flatten the bubbles and then flip the dough. Quickly do the following: Brush the entire top surface of the dough with oil and season with salt and pepper; scatter half the garlic on top, then half the tomatoes, then half the cheese.

Cover the grill and cook the pizza until the edge of the crust is golden and the cheese is melted, 8–10 minutes. The underside of the pizza should be grill-marked but not charred. Transfer to a cutting board. Repeat to grill the second pizza.

In a bowl, whisk together the vinegar, mustard, extra-virgin olive oil, and ½ tsp salt; season to taste with pepper. Add the greens and gently toss.

Top each pizza with the greens, and serve.

25

LEG OF LAMB WITH CHICKPEA, CARROT & RADICCHIO SAUTÉ

serves 4

Here, protein-packed chickpeas, antioxidant–rich carrots, and radicchio simmer in a lemony wine sauce. This bean and vegetable mixture is then served with succulent slices of broiled lamb for a complete meal. For an extra touch of color and nutrition, sprinkle the meat with chopped parsley and serve with a green salad.

2 shallots, minced

2 Tbsp grated lemon zest

1 Tbsp minced fresh rosemary

1¼–1½ lb (625–750 g) boneless leg of lamb, well trimmed

2 Tbsp olive oil, plus more as needed

Salt and freshly ground pepper

4 carrots, halved lengthwise and sliced

1 can (15 oz/470 g) chickpeas, rinsed and drained

1 head radicchio, quartered, cored, and sliced

⅓ cup (3 fl oz/80 ml) dry white wine

⅓ cup (3 fl oz/80 ml) low-sodium chicken broth

1 Tbsp fresh lemon juice

Preheat the broiler. Meanwhile, in a small bowl, mix 3 Tbsp of the shallots, the lemon zest, and rosemary. Place the lamb on a broiler pan, brush all over with oil, and sprinkle generously with salt and pepper. Rub 1½ Tbsp of the shallot-lemon mixture into each side of the lamb. Broil the lamb until a thermometer inserted in the thickest part registers 130°–135°F (54°–57°C) for medium-rare, about 8 minutes per side. Transfer to a warmed platter and tent loosely with foil. Set the pan aside.

In a heavy large frying pan over medium heat, warm the 2 Tbsp oil. Add the remaining shallots and the carrots and sauté until beginning to soften, about 3 minutes. Add the chickpeas and sauté for 3 minutes. Add the radicchio and remaining shallot-lemon mixture and sauté until the radicchio starts to wilt, about 2 minutes.

Set the bottom part of the broiler pan on the stove top over medium heat. Add the wine and bring to a boil, stirring up the browned bits. Add to the chickpeas and boil until the liquid is reduced by half. Add the broth and simmer until nearly dry, about 3 minutes. Mix in the lemon juice and any juices on the platter and season with salt and pepper.

Thinly slice the meat across the grain and serve with the chickpea mixture.

26

CHICKEN CHOPPED SALAD WITH WATERCRESS, CHERRY TOMATOES & OLIVES

serves 4–6

This is a wonderful use for leftover roast chicken, or an inventive way of using a store-bought rotisserie chicken. Cutting each element of the dish into uniform pieces makes an elegant presentation.

2 cups (about 10½ oz/330 g) shredded roasted chicken

2 cups (12 oz/375 g) cherry tomatoes, stemmed and halved lengthwise

1 large cucumber, peeled, halved, seeded, and cut into ½-inch (12-mm) dice

1 bunch watercress, about 5 oz (155 g), tough stems removed and leaves coarsely chopped

¼ lb (125 g) feta cheese, crumbled

2 green onions, chopped

¼ cup (1½ oz/45 g) chopped Kalamata olives

½ cup (4 fl oz/125 ml) extra-virgin olive oil

2 Tbsp fresh lemon juice

1 clove garlic, minced

Salt and freshly ground pepper

In a large bowl, combine the chicken, tomatoes, cucumber, watercress, cheese, green onions, and olives.

In a small bowl, whisk together the oil and the lemon juice until blended. Whisk in the garlic, and season with salt and pepper.

Pour the dressing over the salad mixture, mix gently, and serve.

27

BRINED PORK CHOPS WITH GRILLED STONE FRUIT

serves 6

Grilling stone fruit brings out its natural sweetness and adds appealing grill marks. Plums, peaches, and nectarines are full of vitamins, and antioxidant-rich pitted cherries would make a great substitute as well.

FOR THE PORK BRINE

¼ cup (2 fl oz/60 ml) cider vinegar

¼ cup (2 oz/60 g) firmly packed brown sugar

1 tsp *each* dried thyme and juniper berries

⅛ tsp red pepper flakes

2 Tbsp salt

1 Tbsp freshly ground pepper

6 bone-in pork chops, each at least 1 inch (2.5 cm) thick

Canola oil, for brushing

6 ripe but slightly firm plums, peaches, or nectarines, halved and pitted

To make the pork brine, in a large bowl, combine 6 cups (48 fl oz/1.5 l) water, the vinegar, sugar, thyme, juniper berries, pepper flakes, salt, and pepper and stir until the sugar dissolves.

Place the pork chops in a large locking plastic bag and pour in the brine. Seal the bag, massage the brine around the chops, and refrigerate overnight. Remove the chops from the refrigerator 30 minutes before you plan to begin grilling.

Discard the brine, rinse the chops briefly in cold water, and pat dry with paper towels. Prepare a grill for indirect cooking over medium heat; the temperature inside the grill should be 350°–375°F (180°–190°C). Brush and oil the grill grate.

Place the pork chops on the grill directly over the heat source and sear, turning once, until nicely grill-marked on both sides, 2–3 minutes on each side. Move the chops to the area with no heat, cover the grill, and cook until the chops are somewhat firm to the touch, about 15 minutes for medium, or until an instant-read thermometer inserted horizontally into the center of a chop away from bone registers 145°F (63°C).

Transfer the chops to a platter and let rest for 10 minutes. Meanwhile, brush both sides of the fruit halves with oil and grill over direct heat until grill-marked, about 2 minutes on each side. Serve the pork chops with the grilled fruit alongside.

28

SUMMER VEGETABLE & BULGUR SALAD

serves 4

Choose quick-cooking bulgur to keep the preparation time manageable on a weeknight. Grilling the vegetables keeps the kitchen cool in the summer, but broiling them works just as well. The dressing and bulgur can be made 1 day ahead.

3 Tbsp sherry vinegar

1½ Tbsp Dijon mustard

1 large shallot, minced

¼ cup (2 fl oz/60 ml) extra-virgin olive oil, plus more for brushing

3 Tbsp minced fresh flat-leaf parsley, plus torn leaves for garnish

Salt and freshly ground pepper

1 can (15 oz/470 g) chickpeas, rinsed and drained

1 cup (6 oz/185 g) bulgur

2 *each* red and yellow bell peppers, quartered lengthwise and seeded

3 Asian eggplants, cut lengthwise into thirds

3 zucchini, cut lengthwise into thirds

½ cup (2.5 oz/75 g) crumbled blue cheese

Chopped toasted walnuts for garnish

Prepare a grill for direct-heat cooking over high heat. In a small bowl, stir together the vinegar, mustard, and the shallot. Gradually whisk in ¼ cup (2 fl oz/60 ml) of the oil. Stir in the minced parsley to make a vinaigrette. Season the vinaigrette with salt and pepper. In a large bowl, combine the chickpeas and half of the vinaigrette. Stir to coat. Taste and adjust the seasoning.

In a saucepan, combine the bulgur and 1½ cups (12 fl oz/375 ml) cold water. Season lightly with salt. Bring to a boil, and then reduce the heat to low. Cover and simmer until the bulgur is just tender, 12–15 minutes. Turn off the heat and let the bulgur stand, covered, for at least 5 minutes.

Meanwhile, brush the bell peppers, eggplant, and zucchini with oil, and season with salt and pepper. Arrange the vegetables on the grill rack, cover, and cook until brown in spots, about 7 minutes per side. Transfer the vegetables to a cutting board, cut crosswise into thirds, and then slice lengthwise. Transfer to the bowl with the chickpeas. Add the vinaigrette to taste and toss to coat.

Spoon the bulgur into a large shallow bowl and top with the vegetables. Sprinkle with the cheese, some walnuts, and a few parsley leaves. Serve warm or at room temperature.

29

Here, a classic Southern dish is breaded with whole-wheat panko instead of a heavy batter. Baking the tomatoes still creates the desired crispiness, without the traditional deep-frying step.

OVEN-FRIED GREEN TOMATOES

serves 6

¼ cup (1 oz/30 g) whole-wheat panko bread crumbs

Nonstick cooking spray

¼ cup (1 oz/30 g) grated Parmesan cheese

¼ cup (1½ oz/45 g) yellow cornmeal

1 Tbsp minced fresh flat-leaf parsley

2 tsp fresh thyme leaves

Salt and freshly ground pepper

3 large eggs

½ cup (2½ oz/75 g) all-purpose flour

1 lb (500 g) unripe green tomatoes, cut into slices ½ inch (12 mm) thick

1 cup (8 oz/250 g) part-skim ricotta cheese

1 tsp grated lemon zest

Preheat the oven to 350°F (180°C). Spread the bread crumbs in a small pan and toast in the oven, stirring occasionally, until lightly browned, 6–8 minutes. Transfer to a shallow dish and let cool.

Reduce the oven temperature to 325°F (165°C). Lightly spray a rimmed baking sheet with cooking spray. Add the Parmesan cheese, cornmeal, parsley, and thyme to the cooled bread crumbs and stir to mix. Season with salt and pepper. In another shallow dish, beat the eggs until blended. Place the flour in a third dish.

One at a time, dip the tomato slices into the flour, lightly dusting both sides. Then dip into the eggs and immediately into the crumb mixture, coating both sides well. Place the coated tomato slices slightly apart on the prepared baking sheet. Bake until golden brown on top, about 15 minutes. Turn the slices and continue baking until golden brown on the second side, about 10 minutes longer.

Meanwhile, place the ricotta in a bowl and, using an electric mixer, whip until light and smooth. Mix in the lemon zest and season with salt and pepper.

Transfer the tomatoes to a warmed platter, top each slice with a dollop of the ricotta cream, and serve.

30

White peaches are a bit milder than the red variety, making them a delicious addition to an easy salsa for simple grilled chicken breasts. Serve with a mixture of seasonal lettuces.

GRILLED CHICKEN WITH WHITE PEACH SALSA

serves 4

1½ lb (750 g) skinless, boneless chicken breasts

1 Tbsp olive oil, plus more for grilling

½ tsp chili powder

1 tsp minced fresh thyme

Salt and freshly ground pepper

4 white peaches, peeled (optional), pitted, and coarsely chopped

2 Tbsp fresh lime juice

3 Tbsp finely chopped red onion

Put the chicken in a bowl. Add the oil, chili powder, thyme, ½ tsp salt, and ½ tsp pepper and turn the chicken to coat it well.

Prepare a grill for direct-heat cooking over medium-high heat. Oil the grill rack. Grill the chicken until it has golden brown grill marks, about 2 minutes per side. Cover the grill and cook just until chicken is opaque throughout, 2–3 minutes. Transfer to a platter, tent with foil, and let rest for 5 minutes.

To make the salsa, stir the peaches, lime juice, and onion together in a bowl.

Slice the chicken crosswise and arrange on warmed plates. Spoon the salsa on top of the chicken, and serve.

July is arguably the easiest month to eat healthfully. A wide variety of vegetables grow plump and plentiful under the hot summer sun: sweet corn has its first harvest, juicy peaches overflow in the markets, tomatoes ripen, and summer squash grows in abundance. Concentrate on combining colors and textures to create diversely nutritious meals. Bring new life to old favorites by grilling them, which imparts an appealing smokiness to dishes.

1
GRILLED PIZZA WITH HUMMUS & ROSEMARY SUMMER SQUASH
page 152

2
POACHED SEA BASS WITH TOMATOES & CILANTRO PESTO
page 152

3
MEDITERRANEAN-STYLE CHICKEN VEGETABLE KEBABS
page 154

8
BAKED EGGPLANT ROLLS
page 157

9
TOMATO, ARUGULA & GOAT CHEESE FRITTATA
page 158

10
GARLICKY BLACK BEANS & RICE WITH CORN SALSA
page 158

15
SHRIMP SALAD WITH POTATOES & GREEN BEANS
page 163

16
SUMMER SQUASH NOODLES WITH MINT PESTO
page 163

17
NIÇOISE SALAD WITH SALMON
page 164

22
SMOKY SEA SCALLOPS WITH AVOCADO-CORN SALSA
page 166

23
VEGETABLE MELTS
page 168

24
SMOKY GRILLED CHICKEN & CORN
page 168

29
JERK-SPICED PORK KEBABS WITH PLUM RELISH
page 172

30
SWEET POTATO SALAD
page 172

31
PEPPERCORN TUNA SKEWERS
page 172